The Bible Prophecies Prove Which Church is True

How One Church Fulfilled the Latter-Day Prophecies

Brad Overton

B.Overton Ltd

The Bible Prophecies Prove Which Church is True
How One Church Fulfilled the Latter-Day Prophecies
All Rights Reserved.
Copyright © 2020 Brad Overton
v3.0

The opinions expressed in this manuscript are solely the opinions of the author. The author has represented and warranted full ownership and/or legal right to publish all the materials in this book.

"This material is neither made, provided, approved, nor endorsed by Intellectual Reserve, Inc. or The Church of Jesus Christ of Latter-day Saints. Any content or opinions expressed, implied or included in or with the material are solely those of the owner and not those of Intellectual Reserve, Inc. or The Church of Jesus Christ of Latter-day Saints."

This book may not be reproduced, transmitted, or stored in whole or in part by any means, including graphic, electronic, or mechanical without the express written consent of the publisher except in the case of brief quotations embodied in critical articles and reviews.

B.Overton Ltd

ISBN: 978-0-578-23275-1

Cover Photo © 2020 www.gettyimages.com. All rights reserved - used with permission.

PRINTED IN THE UNITED STATES OF AMERICA

Table of Contents

Introduction	i
One Lord, One Faith, One True Church	1
Ezekiel 4:1-6	7
Why Avoid the Other Versions?	14
The Year Jesus Began His Ministry	17
What Month Jesus Was Born	19
The "Sealed" Prophecies	23
Lining up the "Book of Daniel"	26
Jeremiah 25:12	33
Jeremiah 29:10	36
The Sabbath Years	38
70 Years in Prophecy	40
Daniel 9:24 through Daniel 9:27	41
The "Commandment to Restore"	44

Daniel 9:25	49
Daniel 9:26	51
Daniel 9:27	60
The Desolations	63
The Seventy Weeks in Daniel 9:24	68
Daniel 12:11-12	70
Daniel 12:4 and the "Restoration"	76
Daniel 11:32-34 and the Holy Bible	80
Isaiah 60:1-3 and "Thy Light"	82
Daniel's "Ten Kings"	87
Daniel 2:38-43	89
Daniel 7:3-7	91
Daniel 2:41-42	96
The "Confederation of the Rhine"	101
Daniel 2:44	104
The Sixth Kingdom	107
Daniel 2:34-35	111
The Marriage of the Lamb	113
Daniel's "Sanctuary be Cleansed" Prophecy	121
The "Cleansing" and the "Sanctuary"	128
Prophet Elijah	133

The Blood Sacrifice	139
What Happened in 1844	143
The "Restitution of all Things"	149
Isaiah Chapter 29 King James Version	150
Book of Daniel" Chapter 11 King James Version	182
"Book of Daniel" Chapter 8 King James Version	209
"Book of Daniel" Chapter 7 King James Version	222
Why Jesus waited until he was 30	242
Who was Melchizedek?	245
The Truth about the Rapture	249
Notes	255

Introduction

About 50 years ago, I set out on a spiritual journey, searching for truth, so I could learn as much as possible about Jesus. My spiritual journey not only involved attending many different churches, and denominations, but it also involved listening to the various ministers on television. This is when I noticed that the different churches and ministers, did not agree, concerning how the bible scriptures should be interpreted and taught. How would it be possible to find one church that teaches the gospel truth, in a world filled with so much deceit, and confusion? Many years would pass, before I discovered that the ancient bible prophets provided important prophecies, which could be used to separate God's True Church, from all the rest. Because it would not be possible for more than one church to receive the official authority from God, to teach the gospel, also proves that the authority of God cannot be divided up, and then distributed among the various churches, without dividing the "Kingdom of God" against itself (see KJV Matthew 12:25; Mark 3:24-25; Luke 11:17).

This is confirmed when you fully understand that there is only one correct interpretation of the bible scriptures. Therefore, because so many different denominations misinterpret the bible scriptures, should also explain why so many disagreements continue to spread, throughout the Christian world. As you can see, this brings us right back to the original question, concerning how to find the one church teaching the gospel truth, or in this case, finding one church that would be teaching the one and only correct interpretation of the scriptures. This is where the bible prophecies, concerning the "latter-days," come into play. The bible prophets predicted that God's true church would be established, on earth, sometime during the "last days." Therefore, the most logical way to find this one true church, is to compare the different denominations with the bible prophecies, to see which denomination (if any) fulfilled the "latter-day" prophecies. In other words, we will simply let the bible prophecies prove, which church is true.

One Lord, One Faith, One True Church

THIS BOOK IS quite different, from every other prophecy book on the market today, because this book provides historical evidence, which proves exactly when and how the "latter-day" prophecies were fulfilled. In fact, every prophecy in the "Book of Daniel" has been fulfilled, except for the return of Jesus and Michael ("Michael the Archangel") to begin the judgment (Daniel 12:1-2). The fact that most bible scholars and ministers are still waiting for Daniel's "ten kings" prophecy (Daniel 2:31-43) to be fulfilled, sometime in the future, proves that they cannot explain which church fulfilled the following prophecy:

> **"And in the days of these kings shall the God of heaven set up a kingdom, which shall never be destroyed: and the kingdom shall not be left to other people, but it shall break in pieces and consume all these kingdoms, and it shall stand for ever"** (Daniel 2:44).

Understand; the "Kingdom of God," on earth, is simply another name for Gods True Church. Therefore, because it would not be possible for more than one church to fulfill this "latter-day" prophecy, proves that only one church (God's True Church) is the official "Kingdom of God," on earth, today.

There are two important factors to consider, which will prove whether a bible prophecy was fulfilled, or not:

1. Without exception: every bible prophecy will be fulfilled **on earth.** If this is not true, then the prophecy would not exist, in the bible.

2. The historical record will always explain exactly when and how, the bible prophecy was fulfilled, **on earth.**

The only bible prophecies, which would not meet these two requirements, are prophecies scheduled to be fulfilled, sometime in the future. In other words, every *fulfilled* prophecy will leave behind some historical evidence, which will prove exactly when and how the prophecy was fulfilled. If no historical evidence exists, then this would mean that the prophecy was not fulfilled, or the prophecy was fulfilled in a completely different manner than what people expected. This is what makes the historical records so important. Therefore, to determine exactly when and how the bible prophecies were fulfilled, requires that every prophecy be compared with the historical record. Because this would be a very time-consuming task, for most people to undertake, should explain why this book was written. This book will lead the reader through each bible prophecy, step by step, so the reader can fully understand exactly when and how the prophecy was fulfilled.

However, because so many false interpretations exist, in modern times, also makes it imperative that Christians should learn how to *decipher* the bible prophecies, so they can separate the truth from the falsehoods.

Understand; there is a big difference between "deciphering" the bible prophecies, and "interpreting" what they mean.

To *interpret* a prophecy, simply means to apply your opinion, for what you think the prophecy predicts, or in other words, to make an educated guess.

To *"decipher"* a prophecy, means to "unseal" or to uncover the hidden clues and messages, which exist in most bible prophecies. Only after the prophecy, is accurately deciphered, is when we can learn what the correct interpretation should be.

Even though this may sound rather difficult to accomplish, it is actually a very simple process, which begins with recognizing the hidden clues, which exist within most bible prophecies. Once you learn how to recognize these hidden clues, makes it possible to decipher the prophecy, which in turn, will reveal what the prophecy is predicting. Through this process, you will then recognize whether the correct interpretation was achieved, or not.

Sadly, in modern times, most of these important clues have been overlooked, misconstrued, or in many cases, completely ignored. Keep in mind that these important clues must first be uncovered before the **correct** interpretation can be achieved. As a result, what we learn from the bible prophecies, would depend upon how many of these hidden clues are uncovered, during the deciphering process. The fact that so many false interpretations exist, in modern times, provides proof that very few prophecies have been properly deciphered. Another reason, which explains why so much confusion exists, concerns the fact that we now have over twenty different bible versions, on the market, today. These different versions have opened the door wide, which allow many different and false interpretations to be created, because the bible prophecies do not read the same, in every bible version. Changing just one word, in the bible scriptures, can drastically change the interpretation.

Throughout this book, you will notice that I will often use the phrase, "scheduled to be fulfilled." This terminology is very accurate, simply because when the bible prophecies were originally created, they were more than simple predictions for the future. In many cases, they provided precise timetables, for exactly when certain events were scheduled to happen, on earth. For example: some prophecies talk about the temple, in Jerusalem, and predicted exactly when this temple would be destroyed: prophecies, which were fulfilled, at two different times in history. The historical record proves that these prophecies were fulfilled right on schedule. However, these are not the only prophecies, which contain accurate timetables. In fact, there are many bible prophecies, which were not scheduled to be fulfilled, until sometime during the "last days." Therefore, before these timetables can be uncovered, requires that each bible prophecy be compared with the historical record, so that we can separate the fulfilled prophecies, from the prophecies that remain for the future. It should also be recognized that performing this historical research, would be virtually impossible, without the home computer and the world wide web (www). This is because it would not be possible for any one person, to possess the necessary historical knowledge, to perform this feat.

Because I know that every bible prophecy is true, I have no problem with accepting the premise that every bible prophecy will be fulfilled, on earth, just like the ancient prophets predicted. Therefore, I fail to understand how so many modern-day bible scholars can study the bible prophecies, and at the same time, ignore the different timetables involved. When studying the bible scriptures, we learn that the ancient Israelites received many warnings, concerning future events, which they would eventually have to face. Even though they received these warnings, well ahead of time, many Israelites were still caught off guard, when these predicted events occurred. Why did these people ignore the prophecies, and the signs, that they were given? Believe it or not, this same thing is happening, in modern times. As a result, most Christians are missing out on the fulfillment of several important bible prophecies, today. Why have so many Christians ignored the bible prophecies, and the signs, that they were given? One reason, is because most Christians have not been taught the truth, concerning the "latter-day" prophecies. Therefore, they have no idea how many prophecies have been fulfilled; how many prophecies remain for the future; or even how many prophecies, are in the process of being fulfilled, at this very moment.

It needs to be understood that every bible prophecy is completely accurate, and true, in every respect. Believe it or not, in the prophecy world, this is a very radical statement to make. This is because many modern-day bible scholars have proclaimed that some bible prophecies are not accurate, which means that some bible scriptures must be changed, before the correct interpretation can be achieved. Understand; this whole argument is false, for the simple fact that nothing is wrong with the bible scriptures, or with the bible prophecies. The modern-day bible scholars have created this problem, because they continue to overlook and misconstrue the hidden clues, which reveal exactly how the bible prophecies should be interpreted. Therefore, it would not be possible to correctly interpret any bible prophecy, until after these hidden clues are uncovered, and considered. The fact that every bible prophecy is completely accurate and true, provides proof that the bible prophecies should be handled like an accurate historical record, which was simply recorded in reverse: an accurate historical record, which was recorded, before the actual event occurred.

It needs to be understood that every bible prophecy will be fulfilled, **on earth**, just like the ancient prophets predicted. Therefore, it should also be understood that the prophecy would not exist in the bible, at all, if the prophecy was scheduled to be fulfilled somewhere else. For what purpose would Christians ever need to know about a prophecy, which could never be proven fulfilled, or not? What advantage would a prophecy, of this kind, be to anyone? Therefore, when someone claims that a bible prophecy was fulfilled, then ask them to provide the historical evidence. The historical record will always explain exactly when and how the prophecy was fulfilled. However, if they cannot provide any historical evidence, then this would prove that the prophecy was not fulfilled, or the prophecy was fulfilled in a completely different manner than what many people expected. In either case, the historical record will always prove, when and how the bible prophecy was fulfilled.

There are several things that must be understood, before we can begin, to solve the bible prophecies.

First: it needs to be understood that only the King James Version is being used throughout this discussion. Therefore, if you attempt to follow this discussion, by using another bible version, the prophecies will not read the same way.

Second: the dates presented, throughout this book, are the result of comparing the bible prophecies with the historical record. Therefore, some dates may contradict what is presently taught, today. In either case, the bible prophecies will prove, which dates are accurate, after this deciphering process is completed.

Third: it needs to be remembered that no zero-year existed between the years of 1 B.C. and 1 A.D. Therefore, we must always keep this missing zero-year in mind, when converting the ancient dates, to match our modern-day calendar. As a result, we must add one extra year when calculating from B.C. to A.D., and then subtract one year, when calculating from A.D. to B.C.

Fourth: when the word "days" is used, in bible prophecy, it will often require that we covert the "days" into "years." To demonstrate how this technique was applied, we will now begin our discussion, with Ezekiel's prophecies:

Ezekiel 4:1-6

"For I have laid upon thee the YEARS of their iniquity, ACCORDING TO THE NUMBER OF DAYS, three hundred and ninety DAYS: so shalt thou bear the iniquity of the house of Israel" (Ezekiel 4:5).

NOTICE, THAT IN this prophecy, the number of years were provided as the number of days. This means that we would need to convert the 390 days to 390 years. Therefore, this prophecy predicts that in 390 years (from some unspecified date), **"shalt thou bear the iniquity of the house of Israel."**

Before it would be possible to solve this prophecy, we must first study the "Book of Ezekiel," chapter four, from verses one through six (Ezekiel 4:1-6), while keeping our eyes open for any important hidden clues:

Verse 1: "Thou also, son of man, take thee a TILE, and lay it before thee, and POURTRAY upon it the city, even JERUSALEM:"

Notice that this verse wants us to "pourtray" (or compare), the city of Jerusalem, with a "tile."

Verse 2: "And LAY SIEGE AGAINST IT, and build a fort against it, and cast a mount against it; set the camp also against it, and set battering rams against it round about."

We learn from this verse that Jerusalem will eventually be attacked. Also notice that it will be fortified: **"set battering rams against it round about."**

Verse 3: "Moreover take thou unto thee an IRON PAN, and set it for a WALL OF IRON between thee and the city: and set thy face against it, and IT SHALL BE BESIEGED, and thou shalt lay siege against it. This shall be a sign to the house of Israel."

In this verse, we are told that **"iron pan"** will cause a **"wall of iron,"** which will separate the people in Jerusalem, from God. We are also informed, that Jerusalem will be besieged, which will be a **"sign to the house of Israel."**

Here are the important clues that we uncovered: **tile; pourtray; Jerusalem; lay siege against it; iron pan; wall of iron; it shall be besieged; house of Israel;** and **"according to the number of days."** We were also informed that after Jerusalem is attacked it will then be fortified: **"set battering rams against it round about."** The fact that Jerusalem was scheduled to be fortified, provides proof that Jerusalem would not be completely destroyed, during this attack. Therefore, this prophecy is not talking about the destruction of Jerusalem, which occurred in 70 A.D. For what purpose would it be necessary to fortify a destroyed city?

In verse one, we were instructed to **"pourtray"** (compare) the city of Jerusalem, with **"a tile."** Because tile is often made from clay, which can easily be broken, suggests that Jerusalem was very vulnerable to attack, during this time. In verse two, we then learn that Jerusalem would be attacked: **"lay siege against it,"** and in verse three, we were given a very important clue: **"iron pan,"** which will help identify the person who carried out this attack.

Note: the fact that **"iron pan"** was an ancient Greek god, is a very important clue, which is often misunderstood, in modern times. Because **"iron pan"** was an ancient Greek god, proves that this prophecy was fulfilled, sometime during ancient times when **"iron pan"** was worshipped, by the Greeks and Macedonians. Therefore, we learn from this clue, that the city of Jerusalem was scheduled to be attacked by a Greek, or Macedonian.

Because we did not have an accurate starting date, which we could use to calculate exactly when these 390 years began, forces us to compare this prophecy with the historical record. Therefore, when we study the history of Jerusalem, we discover that Jerusalem was conquered by Ptolemy I Soter, in 321 B.C. Ptolemy I Soter was a very powerful general, who once served under "Alexander the Great," within the "Macedonian-Greek Empire." We learn from the historical record that after Ptolemy I Soter captured Jerusalem, many Israelites were taken to Egypt, and the city was fortified to protect it from further attack. This fulfilled the prophecy: **"set battering rams against it round about."**

This is where the timetables, in verses 4 and 5, come into play:

> **Verse 4: "Lie thou also upon thy left side, and lay the iniquity of the house of Israel upon it: according to the number of the days that thou shalt lie upon it thou shalt bear their iniquity."**
>
> **Verse 5: "For I have laid upon thee the years of their iniquity, according to the number of days, three hundred and ninety days: so shalt thou bear the iniquity of the house of Israel."**

In verse 5, we are told that the **"house of Israel"** would be punished for their **"iniquities"** against God, 390 years later. Because Ptolemy I Soter captured Jerusalem, in 321 B.C., means that we must now add 390 years to 321 B.C. to solve this puzzle. Therefore, calculating forward 390 years from 321 B.C. (or subtract 321 from 390), we end up with 69 A.D. Because we are calculating from B.C. to A.D., we must not forget to add the one missing zero-year, which converts 69 A.D. to 70 A.D. When this prophecy is compared with the historical record, we discover that Jerusalem was attacked in 70 A.D., by the Romans, which resulted in the complete destruction of Jerusalem and the temple. In accordance with verse 5, this is when the nation of Israel was punished, for their "iniquities" against God. They received this great punishment, because they allowed the ancient Greek god **"iron pan"** to be worshipped, in Jerusalem. Also remember that we were informed that this false god would create a "wall of iron," between the people in Jerusalem, and their God: "and set it for a wall of iron between thee and the city."

Note: the reference to **"thee,"** in these scriptures, is often misinterpreted, because many scholars overlook the fact that **"thee"** is referring to the **"son of man"** in verse one, which says: **"Thou also, SON OF MAN, take THEE a tile, and lay it before THEE, and pourtray upon it the city, even Jerusalem."** The **"son of man"** is Jesus Christ (see Daniel 7:13; Matthew 9:6; Mark 2:10; Luke 5:24). Therefore, **"thee"** is not referring to us, at all. The fact that Ezekiel uses the phrase **"son of man,"** provides proof that he already knew about the **"son of man,"** long before Jesus was born.

The mathematics that we performed, confirms that the correct year for when the **"house of Israel"** was scheduled to be punished, was fulfilled in 70 A.D.

Notice that every clue that we needed, to solve these prophecies, were provided in these scriptures, from verses one through five. However, it should also be remembered that these prophecies were written by Ezekiel, who was born in 622 B.C., and died in 570 B.C. This means that Ezekiel was alive when Nebuchadnezzar attacked Jerusalem in 587 B.C. Therefore, Ezekiel was simply warning the **"house of Israel"** that Jerusalem would be attacked again, in 321 B.C., and attacked for a third time 390 years later, in 70 A.D., because of their "iniquities" against God. This is when the people of Israel would receive a great punishment, because they allowed the false god **"iron pan"** to be worshipped, in Jerusalem. The historical record proves that Ezekiel's prophecies were fulfilled, right on schedule, which also proves that his prophecies were completely accurate and true, in every respect.

Note: notice that these interpretations match the clues that we were given. Also notice that we did not have to change any of the words, in the bible scriptures, before we could solve these prophecies. Because these interpretations, passes this test, proves that the correct interpretations were achieved.

With these prophecies solved we will now continue:

> **"And when thou has accomplished them, lie again on the right side, and thou shalt bear the iniquity of the house of Judah forty days: I have appointed thee each day for a year"** (Ezekiel 4:6).

Once again, we are told to convert the days, into years: **"I have appointed thee each day for a year."** However, this time we are being informed: **"thou shalt bear the iniquity of the house of Judah forty days."** In other words, we are being informed that we must now bear the iniquity (bear the wickedness) of Judah, for 40 years. This prophecy is a little more difficult to decipher, simply because we do not have a precise date, to begin our calculations. However, we do have one very important clue, which reveals exactly how to solve this prophecy. This prophecy is basically saying that after we solve the prophecies in verses three, four, and five, that we will then have enough information to solve the prophecy in verse six, by simply following these instructions: **"when thou has accomplished them, lie again on the right side."**

Many scholars fail to interpret this prophecy, simply because they do not understand the relationship that the **"left side"** in verse four, could possibly have with the **"right side,"** in verse six. This verse is simply letting us know that we must reverse our position before we solve this prophecy. In other words, after we solve the prophecies in verses three, four, and five, we must then reverse our calculations so that we can find the secret hidden message, in verse six. Because we determined that 70 A.D. was the correct year, for when Jerusalem would be attacked, this established 70 A.D. as our "left side." With our "left side" established, we must now calculate 40 years ***backwards*** from 70 A.D., to solve this puzzle. Therefore, when we subtract 40 years from 70 A.D., we end up with 30 A.D.

Question: what makes 30 A.D. so important, and what event happened in 30 A.D., which caused the "House of Judah" to be severely punished?

This prophecy begins to make sense, after you fully understand that 30 A.D. was the year, when Jesus began his ministry. Therefore, we learn from this prophecy that the **"house of Judah,"** would be punished 40 years after Jesus begins his ministry, in 30 A.D., because of their **"iniquities"** against God (and Jesus). In other words, the "house of Judah" was severely punished in 70 A.D., because they rejected the "True Gospel of Jesus Christ." As a result, of their iniquities against God, the "house of Israel" and the "house of Judah" were both severely punished, in 70 A.D. Notice that Ezekiel not only predicted exactly when Jerusalem would be attacked, but he also predicted exactly when

Jesus would begin his ministry, approximately 550 years before Jesus was even born. This also confirms that Ezekiel knew that the "son of man" was Jesus Christ.

The actual year, for when Jesus began his ministry, is rather controversial in modern times. This is because most bible scholars have no idea what year Jesus was born; what year he began his ministry; or even what year he was crucified. However, from the prophecies of Ezekiel, we just discovered that Jesus began his ministry in 30 A.D., and then 40 years later, the temple in Jerusalem was destroyed. This is when the **"house of Israel"** and the **"house of Judah"** were both punished, for their *iniquities* against God, and Jesus.

The fact that Ezekiel accurately predicted exactly when Jerusalem would be attacked, twice, provides proof that his prophecies should be handled like an accurate historical record, which was recorded before the actual events occurred.

Why Avoid the Other Versions?

EARLIER, WHEN WE discussed "iron pan," and the fact that "iron pan" was an ancient Greek god, this very important clue opened the door wide, so we could fully understand what Ezekiel predicted. Here is how this prophecy was written in the King James Version (KJV):

> **"Moreover take thou unto thee an iron pan, and set it for a wall of iron between thee and the city: and set thy face against it, and it shall be besieged, and thou shalt lay siege against it. This shall be a sign to the house of Israel"** (Ezekiel 4:3).

The fact that the prophecies do not read the same, in every bible version, should explain why so much confusion exists, concerning how the bible prophecies are interpreted, in modern times.

Here are few examples:

In the New King James Version (NKJV), the words "iron pan" was changed to an "iron plate," which proves that the whole concept that "iron pan" was an ancient Greek god, is completely misunderstood.

In fact, "iron pan" was changed to "iron plate," in the following versions:

New Revised Standard Version (NRSV)
21st century King James Version (KJV21)
New Life Version (NLV)
Christian Standard Bible (CSB)
New Revised Standard Version, Anglicized Catholic Edition (NRSVACE)
New Revised Standard Version Catholic Edition (NRSVCE)
Revised Standard Version (RSV)
The Living Bible (TLB)

As if this is not bad enough, the words "iron pan" was also changed to an 'iron griddle," in the following versions:

English Standard Version (ESV)
New living Translation (NLT)
Complete Jewish Bible (CJB)
Evangelical Heritage Version (EHV)
English Standard Version (ESV)

As you can see, in the examples above, simply changing one little word in the bible scriptures, can drastically change the interpretation. The fact that we now have over fifty different bible versions, written in the English language, should concern every Christian, today. This is because most Christians are completely unaware that many of these versions were intentionally created, to introduce a new and different religious perspective, or theology. For example: some bible versions avoid using the word "master," when their scriptures talk about Jesus, and will only refer to him as a teacher, or a Rabbi, or an instructor. In the "King James Version," Jesus is referred to as "master," approximately 80 times: Matthew 22:36, 23:8, 23:10; Mark 9:5, 12:32, 13:1, 14:45; Luke 3:12, 6:40, 18:18, 19:39; John 11:8, 11:28, 13:13, 13:14. In my opinion, I consider the elimination of this title as an insult against Jesus, which means that I want nothing to do with the other versions, and will only use the King James Version (KJV).

Some bible versions have deleted and changed so many words, it not only makes the prophecies impossible to decipher, but many of the prophecies do not even make any sense. To add more insult to injury, some publishers claim that these scriptural changes were necessary, to make their version more accurate and truthful. It is a very sad fact that we now have more versions of the Holy Bible on earth, today, then what ever existed during the time of King James. Because so many versions existed, during his lifetime, is why he commanded that a new and more accurate version be created. This is how the "King James Version" came into existence. In my opinion, the King James Version (KJV) is the best and most accurate version to use, when studying the scriptures. In fact, it is the only version that can be used, to solve the bible prophecies.

The Year Jesus Began His Ministry

When we studied Ezekiel's prophecies, we discovered that Jesus began his ministry, in 30 A.D. Therefore, we are left with one important question to consider. Is there any proof, that 30 A.D. was the correct year, for when Jesus began his ministry?

When we study the "Book of Luke," and compare Luke 3:1 with Luke 3:21-23, we discover that Jesus was baptized, sometime during the 15th year of Tiberius (15 Tiberius). Here is what we need to know, before we convert 15 Tiberius, to match our modern-day calendar. The first thing to remember, is the fact that after the death of a Caesar, there was a mourning period that lasted for about twelve months. Therefore, the next Caesar would not officially begin his first year in office, until after this twelve-month mourning period is completed. Because Augustus Caesar died in December 14 A.D., proves that the first year of Tiberius did not officially begin until one year later, sometime after December 15 A.D. As a result, the first year that Tiberius Caesar officially began to rule, began in the first month of 16 A.D., which also proves that his 15th year (15 Tiberius) was 30 A.D.

We also learn from Luke that Jesus was about 30 years old when he was baptized (Luke 3:21-23). The fact that Jesus was 30 years old in 15 Tiberius (30 A.D.), and that no zero-year existed between the years of 1 B.C. and 1 A.D., proves that Jesus was born in 1 B.C. As you can see, the bible scriptures have just proven that many modern-day bible scholars are wrong, concerning the year that Jesus was born.

For example: some bible theorists have suggested that Jesus had to be born, sometime before 4 B.C., because King Herod died in 4 B.C. Therefore, they also suggest that the wise men could not have met with King Herod, at any time after 4 B.C. (Matthew 2:1-2). Even though King Herod died, in 4 B.C., these modern-day theorists have overlooked one very important detail. King Herod had two sons named Herod, and after King Herod's death, Herod Archelaus was appointed as the Ethnarch over Judaea. Even though Herod Archelaus never officially received the king title, some historians claim that his military often referred to him, as King Herod. In either case, the wise men would not have known the difference, and therefore, this explains why they reported that they met with King Herod (Matthew 2:1-2). The fact that Jesus was born in 1 B.C., which was three years after the death of King Herod, provides proof that the wisemen met with Herod Archelaus, and not his father.

Sadly, some bible theorists have also suggested that Jesus was crucified in 29 A.D. However, and once again, Luke (Luke 3:21-23) clearly provides proof that their theory is false. How would it be possible for Jesus to be crucified, at the age of 29, when he was baptized at the age of 30?

In either case, we learn from Luke what year Jesus was born, and what year he began his ministry (Luke 3). So which source should we believe? Should we believe some modern-day theorist, who chooses to ignore the bible scriptures, or should we believe the bible, itself?

What Month Jesus Was Born

When we study the "Book of Luke" (Luke 1:26-35), we learn that Mary was visited by an angel, sometime during the sixth month of the year:

> "And in the SIXTH MONTH the angel Gabriel was sent from God unto a city of Galilee, named Nazareth, To a virgin espoused to a man whose name was Joseph, of the House of David; and the virgin's name was Mary. And the angel came in unto her, and said, Hail, thou that art highly favoured, the Lord is with thee: blessed art thou among women. And when she saw him, she was troubled at his saying, and cast in her mind what manner of salutation this should be. And the angel said unto her, Fear not, Mary: for thou hast found favour with God. And, behold, thou shalt conceive in thy womb, and bring forth a son, and shalt call his name JESUS. He shall be great, and shall be called the Son of the Highest: and the Lord God shall give unto him the throne of his father David: And he shall reign over the house of Jacob forever; and of his kingdom there shall be no end. Then said Mary unto the angel, How shall this be, seeing I know not a man? And the angel answered and said

> unto her, The Holy Ghost shall come upon thee, and the power of the Highest shall overshadow thee: therefore also that holy thing which shall be born of thee shall be called the son of God" (Luke 1:26-35).

In the following scriptures, we learn that as soon as Mary discovered that she was pregnant, she visited her cousin Elisabeth, who was about six months pregnant with her son "John the Baptist." This proves that "John the Baptist" was about six months older than Jesus:

> "And it came to pass, that, when Elisabeth heard the salutation of Mary, the babe leaped in her womb; and Elisabeth was filled with the Holy Ghost: And she spake out with a loud voice, and said, Blessed art thou among women, and blessed is the fruit of thy womb" (Luke 1:41-42).

In Hebrew tradition, March (Nissan) was considered as the first month of the year, because this is when spring first begins. Therefore, converting these months to match our modern calendar, means that the sixth month would have been August, and then nine months later Jesus was born. This proves that Jesus was born sometime in April. Therefore, is there any proof that April is accurate?

In the following scriptures, we learn that shepherds were in the field, watching over their flock, during the night:

> "And there were in the same country shepherds abiding in the field, keeping watch over their flock by night" (Luke 2:8).

The shepherds would not have been in the fields, during any of the winter months, for the simple fact that nothing would have been available for the sheep to graze on. However, there would have been plenty of grass in the fields, during the month of April. As you can see, this eliminates December from the picture, completely.

Here is what happened, when an angel appeared to the shepherds, and told them about the birth of Jesus.

> "And, lo, the angel of the Lord came upon them, and the glory of the Lord shone round about them: and they were sore afraid. And the angel said unto them, Fear not: for, behold, I bring you good tidings of great joy, which shall be to all people. For unto you is born this day in the city of David a Saviour, which is Christ the Lord. And this shall be a sign unto you; Ye shall find the babe wrapped in swaddling clothes, lying in a manger. And suddenly there was with the angel a multitude of the heavenly host praising God, and saying, "Glory to God in the highest, and on earth peace, good will toward men." And it came to pass, as the angels were gone away from them into heaven, the shepherds said one to another, Let us now go even unto Bethlehem, and see this thing which is come to pass, which the Lord hath made known unto us. And they came with haste, and found Mary, and Joseph, and the babe lying in a manger. And when they had seen it, they made known abroad the saying which was told them concerning this child. And all they that heard it wondered at those things which were told them by the shepherds. But Mary kept all these things, and pondered them in her heart. And the shepherds returned, glorifying and praising God for all the things that they had heard and seen, as it was told unto them" (Luke 2:9-20).

Note: it is important to notice that Luke never mentions anything about the wise men visiting Mary. In fact, we do not learn anything about the wise men, until Matthew talks about them, and explains that they visited Mary in her house:

"And when they were come into the HOUSE, they saw the young child with Mary his mother, and fell down, and worshipped him: and when they had opened their treasures, they presented unto him gifts; gold, and frankincense, and myrrh" (Matthew 2:11).

Notice that nothing in this scripture reveals exactly how many wise men were present, or how many total gifts that Jesus received, during their visit. We are only told that Jesus received three kinds of gifts: gold, frankincense, and myrrh, but not how many of each kind, Jesus received. This is important, because many churches claim that there were three wise men present, because this is how many gifts that Jesus received that night. However, what happens to their theory if we discover that Jesus received 10 gifts of gold, 10 gifts of frankincense, and 10 gifts of Myrrh? Would we then have to conclude that thirty wise men were also present? I bring this up, to prove that we have been taught many false things, concerning our Christian beliefs, which is based more upon tradition, rather than the truth. In fact, we were previously warned to keep our eyes open, for the false ministers and teachers who would teach these fables:

"For the time will come when they will not endure sound doctrine; but after their own lusts shall they heap to themselves TEACHERS, having itching ears; And they shall turn away their ears from the truth, and shall be turned unto fables" (2 Timothy:3-4).

If the ministers (teachers) are not teaching the truth about the birth of Jesus, then what else are they teaching, which is not based upon the gospel truth?

And this is where Daniel's "sealed" prophecies come into play.

The "Sealed" Prophecies

ONE REASON, WHICH explains why so many false interpretations exist, in modern times, is because many bible prophecies were "sealed." Even though this "sealing" process is only mentioned in the "Book of Daniel," this "sealing" process was also applied to many other bible prophecies, to keep the correct interpretations hid, until after the "last days" arrived: **"till the time of the end."**

> **"And he said, Go thy way, Daniel: for the words are closed up and sealed TILL THE TIME OF THE END"** (Daniel 12:9).

The fact that Daniel was told that his prophecies would remain **"closed up and sealed TILL the time of the end,"** reveals that something important was scheduled to happen, during **"the time of the end,"** which would allow his prophecies to be "unsealed." This important event was the arrival of the home computer with the world-wide web (www). This technology now makes it possible to compare, the ancient bible prophecies, with the historical records.

Note: it needs to be understood that the bible prophecies discussed, throughout this book, were researched between the years of 1999 and

2000, while the internet was still in its infancy. Therefore, most of this research was completed, before the internet was filled up with a lot of worthless information, and commercial advertisements. I dare say, that if I attempted to perform this research today, it would be almost impossible to accomplish. Nevertheless, it was the home computer with the world wide web (www), which allowed the prophecies of Daniel (and many others) to be "unsealed." The fact that we are living on earth, during the "last days," when many of the "latter day" prophecies were scheduled to be fulfilled, should be a wake-up call for every Christian, to get prepared:

> **"For yourselves know perfectly that the day of the Lord so cometh as a thief in the night** (1 Thessalonians 5:2).

How would it be possible for Christians to get prepared, when most Christians cannot separate the truth from the falsehoods, being taught in modern times? In the "New Testament," we were warned that many divisions would occur, within the Christian community:

> **"Salute one another with an holy kiss. The churches of Christ salute you. Now I beseech you, brethren, mark them which cause DIVISIONS and offences contrary to the doctrine which ye have learned; AND AVOID THEM. For they that are such serve not our Lord Jesus Christ, but their own belly; and by good words and fair speeches deceive the hearts of the simple"** (Romans 16:16-18).

We see the result of these divisions, today, because the Christian denominations cannot even agree, concerning how the bible scriptures should be interpreted and taught. Think about it! These divisions would not exist, if every Christian denomination interpreted the bible scriptures, correctly. We would not have thousands of different denominations, teaching thousands of different opinions, and interpretations.

The fact that the Christian churches are divided, should also explain why so much confusion exists, in modern times. These false interpretations not only keep the different denominations divided, but they also keep many Christians from recognizing the Real Truth, when they hear it for the first time. However, there is one thing that Christians can do, to help clear up some of this confusion. Every Christian should study the bible prophecies, so they can learn what the ancient prophets predicted, concerning our "latter days." Many of these prophecies are simple road maps, designed to help the "latter day" Christians, find the right path. The hidden clues reveal exactly how the bible prophecies should be deciphered, and from there, Christians will then learn what the correct interpretations should be.

Lining up the "Book of Daniel"

SOMETIME DURING 2000, after studying the "Book of Daniel," it suddenly occurred to me that something was wrong. This is when I began to notice that some of the chapters, in the "Book of Daniel," appeared to be out of order. For example: chapters 5, 6, 7, and 8 were out of order, for the simple fact that King Belshazzar was still alive in chapters 7 and 8, even though he was killed in chapter 5 (Daniel 5:30). Because this would be impossible, I then decided to line up the chapters in the correct order, by using the succession of the kings. This was possible, because Daniel talks about four different kings: Nebuchadnezzar, Belshazzar, Cyrus, and Darius. Because chapters one through four, talks about Nebuchadnezzar, confirmed that these four chapters held the correct position. The fact that chapters five, seven, and eight talks about Belshazzar, confirms that these three chapters should immediately follow chapter four. Because chapters six, nine, and eleven talks about Darius, confirms that these chapters were next. And because Michael ("Michael the Archangel") is only mentioned in chapters 10 and 12, provides proof that these two chapters are directly connected. Because chapter 12 talks about the final days, on earth, confirms that this chapter should remain in the last position.

Understand; it is very important to line up these chapters, in the correct order, so we can determine exactly when Daniel received these prophecies. The fact that many historians claim that no record of "Darius the Median" exists, made it imperative that I should solve this simple puzzle, and then reveal the identity of "Darius the Median," before discussing Daniel's prophecies.

"Darius the Median"

In chapter nine (Daniel 9:1), we learn that Daniel received the prophecies in this chapter, during "the first year of Darius the "son of Ahasuerus."

"In the first year of Darius the son of Ahasuerus, of the seed of the Medes, which was made king over the realm of the Chaldeans" (Daniel 9:1).

The reference to **"the son of Ahasuerus"** was rather puzzling, until I realized that "Ahasuerus" was possibly a name (or title) for some ancient ancestor of "Cambyses I," who was the father of "Cyrus the Great." It is interesting to note that the identity of "Darius the Mede" (also "Darius the Median"), continues to puzzle many modern-day scholars, because they claim that no historical record exists, which mentions anything about "Darius the Mede." As a result, many bible scholars have declared that because this name is wrong, provides proof that the entire "Book of Daniel" is not accurate. In other words, they choose to blame the entire "Book of Daniel" because they have failed to solve the simple puzzle, concerning "Darius the Mede." The reason why most bible scholars fail to solve this simple puzzle, is because they continue to overlook the important clues, which Daniel provided.

In the following scripture, we learn that "Darius the Median" was 62 years old, when Babylon was conquered:

> "And Darius the Median took the kingdom, being about threescore and two years old" (Daniel 5:31).

This scripture eliminates "Darius I" completely, because he was born in 550 B.C., which proves that he was about 12 years old, when Babylon was conquered in 538 B.C.

The "Book of Daniel" refers to Cyrus as the **"prince of the kingdom of Persia,"** when God proclaims: **"But the prince of the kingdom of Persia withstood me one and 20 days"** (Daniel 10:13). When we convert these twenty-one days into years, and then subtract twenty-one years from 559 B.C. (the year when Cyrus succeeded his father), we end up with 538 B.C. Notice that this is the same year when Cyrus conquered Babylon. When we subtract 538 B.C. from 600 B.C. (when Cyrus was born), we discover that "Cyrus the Great" was 62 years old, during that time. Notice that this is the same age, as "Darius the Median," in Daniel 5:31, above.

Therefore, we now have two clues, which proves that Cyrus was "Darius the Median." The first clue was the fact that "Darius the Mede," was **"the son of Ahasuerus,"** referring to an ancient ancestor of "Cambyses I." We also learn from the second clue that Cyrus was 62 years old, when Babylon was captured, in 538 B.C. This Median title begins to make sense when you understand that the Medes were in control, when Cyrus succeeded his father, in 559 B.C. This is when Cyrus received his Median title as the "King of the Medes." Therefore, the person who captured Babylon, was the same individual who Daniel recognized as "Darius the Median." This proves that "Darius" was some ancient title, which Cyrus received, when he first began to rule over the Median Empire: just like the Romans used their title of "Caesar."

There is one more important clue, mentioned in chapter 11, which provides proof that "Darius the Median" was Cyrus, and no one else:

"And now will I shew thee the truth. Behold, there shall stand up yet three kings in Persia; and the fourth shall be far richer than they all: and by his strength through his riches he shall stir up all against the realm of Grecia" (Daniel 11:2).

In accordance with this prophecy, we are told that three more Persian kings would follow the reign of King Cyrus, and that the fourth king: **"shall stir up all against the realm of Grecia."** This prophecy is talking about the kings, who once ruled over the "Achaemenid Empire," which began in 550 B.C. and ended in 330 B.C. However, at first glance, it appears that something is wrong with this prophecy. This is because the historical record proves that thirteen more kings, ruled over this empire, after the death of "Cyrus the Great." Understand; this prophecy is only predicting that three more kings would be named "Darius," after the rule of this "Darius the Median" ("Darius 0"), is over. These three kings were "Darius I," "Darius II," and "Darius III." We also learn that the fourth king (Darius III), would fight a war against Grecia: referring to the "Macedonian-Greek Empire." This prophecy not only proves that King Cyrus was "Darius the Median" ("Darius 0"), but it also proves that the fourth and last "Darius" was "Darius III," who fought a war against the "Macedonian-Greek Empire," fulfilling the prophecy: **"and the fourth shall be far richer than they all: and by his strength through his riches he shall stir up all against the realm of Grecia"** (Daniel 11:2).

Notice that the "Book of Daniel" accurately predicted that three more kings would receive the "Darius" title, after the death of "Cyrus the Great" ("Darius 0"), which was several years before two of these kings were even born. This provides proof that the "Book of Daniel" is completely accurate, and true, which should also be handled like an accurate historical record that was recorded in reverse: before the predicted events occurred.

Because we now understand that "Darius the Median," was Cyrus, and that Cyrus was also a Persian King, provides proof that the following verse is true:

> **"So this Daniel prospered in the reign of Darius, and in the reign of Cyrus the Persian"** (Daniel 6:28).

In other words, when Cyrus conquered Babylon, he arrived on the scene as "Darius the Median." Sometime later, after Cyrus defeated the Median Empire, is when Cyrus began to rule over his kingdom as "Cyrus the Persian." Therefore, Daniel is simply confirming that he prospered under both titles, that "Cyrus the Great" received.

This also explains why Daniel made the following statement:

> **"Also I in the first year of Darius the Mede, even I, stood to confirm and to strengthen him"** (Daniel 11:1).

Understand; Daniel would not have made this statement, if "Darius the Mede," was his enemy.

The fact that King Nebuchadnezzar was also a Chaldean King (Ezra 5:12), when he ruled over Babylon, explains why Cyrus became the **"king over the realm of the Chaldeans,"** after he defeated the "Babylonian Empire."

Therefore, this proves that verse one, in chapter nine, was true:

> **"In the FIRST YEAR of Darius the son of Ahasuerus, of the seed of the Medes, which was made king over the realm of the Chaldeans"** (Daniel 9:1).

Notice that this verse confirms that **"Darius the son of Ahasuerus,"** was Cyrus, because Cyrus became the **"king over the realm of the Chaldeans,"** when he captured Babylon.

Because Daniel received the prophecies, in chapter 9, during the first year that Cyrus ruled over Babylon, proves that he received these prophecies in 538 B.C.

This is also true concerning, chapter 11, because Daniel says:

> **"Also I in the FIRST YEAR of Darius the Mede, even I, stood to confirm and to strengthen him"** (Daniel 11:1).

This proves that Daniel received the prophecies, in chapters 9 and 11, in 538 B.C.

However, when we study verse one, in chapter 10, we discover that Daniel did not receive the scriptures in chapter 10, until the **third year** that Cyrus ruled over Babylon:

> **"In the THIRD YEAR of Cyrus king of Persia a thing was revealed unto Daniel, whose name was called Belteshazzar; and the thing was true, but the time appointed was long: and he understood the thing, and had understanding of the vision"** (Daniel 10:1).

Because the first year that Cyrus ruled over Babylon, was 538 B.C., proves that the third year was 536 B.C. Therefore, Daniel did not receive the scriptures in chapter 10, until two years after he received the scriptures in chapters 9 and 11. As a result, this proves that the verse in chapter 10, which reads: **"Now I am come to make thee understand what shall befall thy people in the latter days: for yet the vision is for many days"** (Daniel 10:14), was not talking about any prophecies that Daniel previously received, in chapter 11.

The fact that the "Book of Daniel" is not lined up in the proper order, is a very startling revelation, in modern times. This is because many Christian ministers have used verse 14, in chapter 10 (Daniel 10:14), to prove to their congregations that the prophecies in chapter 11, are prophecies for the future. However, it was just proven that Daniel received chapter 10, two years after he received the prophecies in chapter 11, which proves that many ministers are wrong. Even though Daniel did receive the promise: **"Now I am come to make thee understand what shall befall thy people in the latter days: for yet the vision is for many days"** (Daniel 10:14), this scripture is talking about the "latter day" prophecies in chapter 12, and not any prophecies that Daniel previously received in chapter 11. The fact that Michael ("Michael the Archangel") is mentioned, in the last verse of chapter 10, and in the first verse in chapter 12, proves that these two chapters are directly connected. Therefore, chapter 10 is simply the introduction for chapter 12, which contains prophecies for the **"latter days."**

Therefore, for studying purposes, the chapters in the "Book of Daniel" should be lined up, in the following order:

    King Nebuchadnezzar chapters 1, 2, 3, 4
    King Belshazzar chapters 8, 7, 5
    King Cyrus and "Darius the Median," chapter 6, 9, 11
    "Michael the Archangel," chapter 10
    "Michael the Archangel," and the "latter days," chapter 12

JEREMIAH 25:12

IN THE FOLLOWING scripture, we learn that Daniel studied the prophecies of Jeremiah, and this is when he discovered that the Israelites were scheduled to be released from their Babylonian captivity, in 538 B.C.

> **"In the first year of his reign I Daniel understood by books the number of the years, whereof the word of the Lord came to Jeremiah the prophet, that he would accomplish seventy years in the desolations of Jerusalem"** (Daniel 9:2).

This is where Jeremiah's prophecy comes into play:

> **"And it shall come to pass, when seventy years are accomplished, that I will punish the king of Babylon, and that nation, saith the Lord, for their iniquity, and the land of the Chaldeans, and will make it perpetual desolations"** (Jeremiah 25:12).

The key in deciphering this prophecy, is to understand that the seventy years mentioned, is an actual seventy years of time. We learn from this prophecy that in 70 years (from some unspecified date), the King of Babylon and his nation would be punished, and the land of the

Chaldeans would cease to exist, from that time forward: meaning of **"perpetual desolations."** Therefore, when this prophecy is compared with the history of the Babylonian Empire, we discover exactly when this prophecy was scheduled to be fulfilled.

QUESTION: WHEN DID THESE 70 YEARS BEGIN?

When studying the historical record, we learn that the Babylonians, the Medes, and the Persians formed an alliance to fight against the Assyrians. In 608 B.C., the Babylonians successfully conquered the city of Harran, which was the capital city of the Assyrian Empire. This prophecy correlates this successful attack, with the beginning of the Babylonian Empire, itself. As a result, and in accordance with Jeremiah's prophecy (Jeremiah 25:12), the Babylonian Empire would then be severely punished 70 years later, and this is also when the land of the Chaldeans would cease to exist.

Therefore, when we calculate forward seventy years from 608 B.C., we end up with 538 B.C. Notice that this is the same year that "Cyrus the Great" conquered Babylon. This not only ended the seventy-year reign, of the Babylonian Empire, but it also freed the Israelites from their seventy-years of captivity. These calculations also confirm that Cyrus conquered Babylon in 538 B.C.

The second part of this prophecy (Jeremiah 25:12), concerning the land of the Chaldeans, and how this land would cease to exist: **"perpetual desolations,"** is a little more challenging to decipher, until you realize that the King of Babylon is also a Chaldean King (Ezra 5:12). Therefore, when "Cyrus the Great" conquered Babylon, he also conquered the land of the Chaldeans, which is when he began to rule over the Chaldeans: **"In the FIRST YEAR of Darius the son of Ahasuerus, of the seed of the Medes, which was made KING OVER THE REALM OF THE CHALDEANS"** (Daniel 9:1).

Therefore, because the prophecy of Jeremiah (Jeremiah 25:12) was fulfilled in 538 B.C., provides more proof that the bible prophecies are completely accurate and true, in every respect.

Jeremiah 29:10

These same 70 years are mentioned, again, in the following prophecy:

> **"For thus saith the Lord, That after SEVENTY YEARS be accomplished at Babylon I will visit you, and perform my good word toward you, in causing you to return to this place"** (Jeremiah 29:10).

Before we proceed, it needs to be understood that Jeremiah received this prophecy, when he was in Jerusalem (Jeremiah 29:1). Therefore, this prophecy is simply letting him know, that after Babylon is conquered in 538 B.C., that there will be an important reason for the Israelites to return to Jerusalem: **"in causing you to return to this place."** This important reason was to rebuild the temple in Jerusalem. This prophecy was scheduled to be fulfilled, after the Israelites seventy years of captivity, comes to an end: **"after seventy years be accomplished at Babylon.** The Israelites were freed from their captivity, after the Babylon Empire was conquered in 538 B.C., which was precisely 70 years after the city of Harran was conquered, in 608 B.C. After the Israelites were freed, the Israelites began to return to Jerusalem, so they could rebuild their temple. This is when Cyrus signed the first decree, concerning the rebuilding of the temple, in Jerusalem:

"In the first year of Cyrus the king the same Cyrus the king made a decree concerning the house of God at Jerusalem, Let the house be builded, the place where they offered sacrifices, and let the foundations thereof be strongly laid; the height thereof threescore cubits, and the breadth thereof threescore cubits" (Ezra 6:3).

The Sabbath Years

In this prophecy, we learn exactly when the second temple, in Jerusalem, was scheduled to be rebuilt:

> **"To fulfil the word of the Lord by the mouth of Jeremiah, until the land had enjoyed her Sabbaths: for as long as she lay desolate she kept Sabbath, to fulfil threescore and ten years"** (2 Chronicles 36:21).

The most important clue that we need, to solve this prophecy, concerns the sabbatical year, which means that every seventh year the land was required to rest. This sabbatical law is explained in the books of Exodus and Leviticus:

> **"But the SEVENTH YEAR thou shalt let it rest and lie still; that the poor of thy people may eat: and what they leave the beasts of the field shall eat. In like manner thou shalt deal with thy vineyard, and with thy olive yard"** (Exodus 23:11).

> **"But in the SEVENTH YEAR shall be a sabbath of rest unto the land, a sabbath for the Lord: thou shalt neither sow thy field, nor prune thy vineyard"** (Leviticus 25:4).

There is another important clue, which concerns the word "desolate," and how this word should be applied to this prophecy: **"for as long as she lay desolate she kept sabbath"** (2 Chronicles 36:21). Spiritually speaking, when the bible talks about the land in Jerusalem (or Israel) being "desolate," this often means that the temple in Jerusalem, does not exist. Therefore, in accordance with this prophecy, Jerusalem was scheduled to obey the "sabbath of rest" for a total of 70 years (20 times 3 plus 10 equals 70 years). This means that the 70 years of the "sabbath of rest" began, as soon as the first temple in Jerusalem was destroyed by Nebuchadnezzar, in 587 B.C. Therefore, the second temple was not scheduled to be rebuilt, until after the "sabbath of rest" is completed, which would be 70 years from 587 B.C. The historical record proves that the temple was rebuilt, in 517 B.C., which was precisely 70 years after Nebuchadnezzar destroyed the temple, in 587 B.C. Therefore, the **"sabbath of rest unto the land"** was fulfilled in 517 B.C., just like this prophecy predicted.

70 Years in Prophecy

Here is a list of four different seventy-years to remember:

1. The Babylonian Empire was scheduled to remain in power for a total of 70 years: calculated from 608 B.C. to 538 B.C.

2. The children of Israel were predicted to remain in captivity for a total of 70 years: also calculated from 608 B.C. to 538 B.C. Their captivity began when the Babylonian Empire captured the capital city of Harran, in 608 B.C., and ended when "Cyrus the Great" conquered the Babylonian Empire, in 538 B.C.

3. The second temple in Jerusalem was scheduled to be rebuilt, in 517 B.C., which was precisely 70 years after Nebuchadnezzar destroyed the first temple, in 587 B.C.

4. The second temple in Jerusalem was scheduled to be destroyed, 70 years after the birth of Jesus, and 40 years after Jesus began his ministry in 30 A.D.

Note: this last 70 years, is often overlooked by most modern-day ministers, because they have no idea what year Jesus was born, or what year Jesus began his ministry.

Daniel 9:24 through Daniel 9:27

Before we begin to solve, the next set of prophecies, it needs to be remembered that the same rules still apply. When necessary we will convert the days into years, and then add or subtract the one missing zero-year, when necessary.

Earlier I mentioned that the "Book of Daniel," was "sealed," and that the chapters were not lined up in the proper order. This was done to keep the correct interpretations hid until after the "last days" arrived. This same tactic was also applied to the following four prophecies, which explains why they are not lined up in the correct order, or in accordance with the actual series of events. This will become clear after these prophecies are deciphered.

Before we attempt to solve these prophecies, from Daniel 9:24 through Daniel 9:27, we must first find an accurate date to begin our calculations. Therefore, we must skip over verse twenty-four, and begin our research with verse twenty-five, which says:

> **"Know therefore and understand, that from the going forth of the commandment to restore and to build Jerusalem unto**

the messiah the prince shall be seven weeks, and threescore and two weeks: the street shall be built again, and the wall, even in troublous times"** (Daniel 9:25).

At first glance, this prophecy appears to be rather complicated, but it becomes a lot easier to understand, after this prophecy is divided in the following manner:

1. **"That from the going forth of the commandment to restore."**
2. **"to build Jerusalem unto the Messiah the prince,"**
3. **"shall be seven weeks, and threescore and two weeks."**
4. **"the street shall be built again, and the wall, even in troublous times."**

We learn from this prophecy that three different events were scheduled to happen. Notice that the first two events are separated by a total of 69 weeks (7 plus 60, plus 2 equals 69). When these 69 weeks are converted into days (69 times 7 equals 483) they equal 483 years. Therefore, before we can decipher this prophecy, we must first determine exactly when these 483 years began. The key that we will now use to solve this puzzle, concerns the actual year that the **"going forth of the commandment to restore,"** was officially placed in force. From that point it becomes a very simple task of calculating, exactly when the next prophecy: **"to build Jerusalem unto the Messiah the prince,"** was scheduled to be fulfilled.

The **"commandment to restore"** is referring to the official document, which authorized the confiscated items, which were previously taken from the temple by Nebuchadnezzar (in 587 B.C.), to be returned ("restored") to the people in Jerusalem (Ezra 7:11-26). This edict was originally signed by King Cyrus (Ezra 6:1-22) in 538 B.C., but was never officially placed in force, because the temple rebuilding program was delayed. Several years later, King "Artaxerxes I" signed this same document, in 458 B.C., and then delivered this important document to "Ezra the priest." This is when this important document began its long journey, which would allow the second temple in Jerusalem to be "restored," when the items that were previously removed from the first temple, by Nebuchadnezzar in 587 B.C., would be "restored" (returned) to the people in Jerusalem.

When studying the bible scriptures, concerning this temple rebuilding program, we learn that during the reign of "King Cyrus," the inhabitants of the land often interfered with the construction of the temple, which caused the construction to stop (Ezra 4:4). Several years later, in 517 B.C., during the reign of "Darius the Great," the temple was successfully rebuilt, even though the inhabitants of the land continued to interfere with its construction. This is when Daniel's prophecy, concerning the rebuilding of the temple in Jerusalem, comes into play. Notice that Daniel predicted that **"the street shall be built again, and the wall, even in troublous times"** (Daniel 9:25). The **"troublous times,"** is referring to the interference by the inhabitants, which often delayed the temple construction. Even though these **"troublous times"** continued, the temple was successfully rebuilt, in 517 B.C.

The "Commandment to Restore"

We learn from the bible scriptures that "Ezra the priest" first arrived, in Jerusalem, during the seventh year of the King:

> **"And he came to Jerusalem in the fifth month, which was in the seventh year of the king"** (Ezra 7:8).

Because "King Artaxerxes I" ruled over the Persian Empire, between the years of 464 B.C. to 425 B.C., proves that the first year was 464 B.C, which also proves that the seventh year was 458 B.C.

We learn from the scriptures that on the first day, of the first month, Ezra left Babylon: and on the first day, of the fifth month, he arrived in Jerusalem:

> **"For upon THE FIRST DAY OF THE FIRST MONTH began he to go up from Babylon, and on THE FIRST DAY OF THE FIFTH MONTH came he to Jerusalem, according to the good hand of his God upon him"** (Ezra 7:9).

From the following scriptures, we learn that Ezra made this trip, for one specific purpose:

> "For Ezra had prepared his heart to seek the law of the Lord, and to do it, and to teach in Israel statutes and judgments" (Ezra 7:10).

However, it should also be remembered that Ezra did not have the "commandment to restore" document in his hands, during this time. In accordance with chapter eight, we learn that Ezra arrived in Jerusalem for a second time, after he left the river Ahava on the twelfth day of the first month:

> "Then we departed from the river of Ahava on the TWELFTH DAY OF THE FIRST MONTH, to go unto Jerusalem: and the hand of our God was upon us, and he delivered us from the hand of the enemy, and of such as lay in wait by the way" (Ezra 8:31).

Notice that this is when Ezra delivered the "commandment to restore" document, into the hands of the governors, and lieutenants:

> "And they delivered the king's commissions unto the king's lieutenants, and to the governors on this side the river: and they furthered the people, and the house of God." (Ezra 8:36).

Question: when did Ezra receive this **"commandment to restore"** document in his hands?

When we calculate from the time that Ezra arrived in Jerusalem, on the first day of the fifth month, to when he left the river Ahava, on the twelfth day of the first month, we discover that a total of eight months are missing. These missing months are easily accounted for, when you understand that a round trip from Babylon to Jerusalem, took approximately eight months to accomplish. Therefore, because Ezra did not have the "commandment to restore" document in his hands, when he arrived in Jerusalem the first time, also meant that he had to make another trip to Babylon, so that he could receive this important document from the king. In accordance with the following scriptures, a one-way trip took approximately four months, to accomplish:

"For upon the FIRST DAY OF THE FIRST MONTH began he to go up from Babylon, and on the FIRST DAY OF THE FIFTH MONTH came he to Jerusalem, according to the good hand of his God upon him" (Ezra 7:9).

This means that Ezra did not arrive in Jerusalem, with this important document in his hands, until approximately eight months later: eight months after he arrived, in Jerusalem, the first time. To make this easier to understand, we will now convert these ancient dates, to match our modern-day calendar.

Note: in accordance with Hebrew tradition, we will begin these calculations with the month of March, which was Nissan, the first month in the Hebrew calendar. Nissan was chosen, as their first month, because March is when spring first begins.

Therefore, on the first day of the first month, March 1, 458 B.C., Ezra left Babylon (Ezra 7:8). On the first day of the fifth month, July 1, 458 B.C., Ezra arrived in Jerusalem for the first time (Ezra 7:8). Approximately four months later, possibly sometime around November 1, 458 B.C., Ezra arrived in Babylon. This is when Ezra received the "restore" document from the king. Approximately four months later, on March 12, 457 B.C., Ezra left the river Ahava, and arrived in Jerusalem for the second time (Ezra 8:31). This is when Ezra delivered this important document into the hands of the proper authorities (Ezra 8:36). Notice that the missing eight months are easily accounted for. Also notice that the year, Ezra arrived in Jerusalem for the second time, was 457 B.C.

Note: these calculations do not change when we begin these calculations with the first month as January 1, 458 B.C., the fifth month as May 1, and four months later as September 1, 458 B.C., which would mean that Ezra arrived in Jerusalem, four months later on January 12, 457 B.C. In both cases, the trip started in 458 B.C. and ended in 457 B.C.

With these times calculated, we will now continue our discussion, beginning with verse thirty-six, which proclaims: **"And they delivered the king's commissions to the king's lieutenants, and to the governors"** (Ezra 8:36).

When this document was officially delivered into the hands of the lieutenants and governors, this document ordered the officials to perform their duties, and return (**"restore"**) the confiscated items back into the hands of the people, in Jerusalem. This was the year that Daniel was referring to as**: "that from the going forth of the commandment to restore"** (Daniel 9:25), which started the clock, that we will now use to calculate our 69 weeks.

Understand; the calculations that we previously performed, proves that 458 B.C. was the correct year, for when "Ezra the priest" received the edict from the king. However, it needs to be remembered that Ezra did not arrive in Jerusalem, with this document in his hands, until 457 B.C. (Ezra 8:31). Therefore, 457 B.C. was the correct year, for when this edict was officially placed in force, for this is when the lieutenants and governors received this important document, in their hands.

Note: keep 457 B.C. in mind, because we will use this year again, to solve a few more prophecies. In fact, another prophecy will confirm that 457 B.C. was the correct year, for when this important document was officially placed in force.

Daniel 9:25

THEREFORE, WE WILL now use 457 B.C., to decipher the following:

> "Know therefore and understand, that from the going forth of the commandment to restore and TO BUILD JERUSALEM UNTO THE MESSIAH THE PRINCE shall be seven weeks, and threescore and two weeks: the street shall be built again, and the wall, even in troublous times" (Daniel 9:25).

Understand; the prophecy: **"to build Jerusalem unto the messiah the prince,"** is referring to the ministry of "John the Baptist," who received a special "calling" and priesthood duty: **"to prepare ye the way of the Lord"** (Isaiah 40:3; Matthew 3:1-3; Luke 3:2-4; Mark 1:1-4). Therefore, it was the ministry of "John the Baptist," which prepared the people in Jerusalem, for the arrival of their Messiah:

> **"The voice of him that crieth in the wilderness, Prepare ye the way of the Lord, make straight in the desert a highway for our God"** (Isaiah 40:3).

> **"In those days came JOHN THE BAPTIST, preaching in

> the wilderness of Judaea, And saying, Repent ye: for the kingdom of heaven is at hand. For this is he that was spoken of by the prophet Esias, saying, The voice of one crying in the wilderness, Prepare ye the way of the Lord, make his paths straight" (Mathew 3:1-3).

In accordance with Daniel's prophecy (Daniel 9:25), it was "John the Baptist" who fulfilled the prophecy: to **"build Jerusalem unto the Messiah."** This means that John would **"build"** up membership in the Church of Jesus Christ. It was during the ministry of "John the Baptist," when he began to preach repentance, and baptized the people who believed in Jesus. This is when the **"seven weeks, and threescore and two weeks"** come into play. Therefore, from the time that **"the commandment to restore"** document was officially placed in force, to when "John the Baptist" began his ministry, was a total of 69 weeks, calculated 483 years from 457 B.C. This equals 26 A.D., and because we are calculating from B.C. to A.D., we must not forget to add the one missing zero-year, which converts 26 A.D. to 27 A.D. Therefore, from this prophecy, we learn that "John the Baptist" began his ministry, in 27 A.D.

With this prophecy solved we will now continue:

Daniel 9:26

"And after threescore and two weeks shall Messiah be cut off, but not for himself: and the people of the prince that shall come shall destroy the city and the sanctuary; and the end thereof shall be with a flood, unto the end of the war desolations are determined" (Daniel 9:26).

TO MAKE THIS prophecy easier to understand, we will now divide this verse, in the following manner:

1. "And after threescore and two weeks shall Messiah be cut off, but not for himself."
2. "and the people of the prince that shall come shall destroy the city and the sanctuary."
3. "and the end thereof shall be with a flood, unto the end of the war desolations are determined."

At first glance, it appears that this prophecy is talking about one important event, which was scheduled to happen, in threescore and two weeks (62 weeks), or 434 years. This is when the prophecy, concerning the **"Messiah be cut off, but not for himself,"** would be fulfilled. However, this is not what this prophecy is predicting, at all. In fact, this prophecy is only creating an accurate timetable, for approximately when three different prophecies would be fulfilled, sometime *after* a total of 62 weeks (434 years) have passed. Therefore, when we calculate 434 years from 457 B.C., we end up with 23 A.D., and when we add the one missing zero-year, we end up with 24 A.D. In other words, these three prophecies will not begin to be fulfilled, until sometime *after* 24 A.D.:

1. Messiah will be "cut off."
2. The "city and the sanctuary" will be destroyed.
3. And the "Desolations" will take place after the "war."

Therefore, sometime after 24 A.D., Jesus will be killed ("cut off"): Jerusalem and the temple will be destroyed: and after this war is over, the desolations (referring to the "abomination of desolations") will begin to spread, around the world.

The reference to **"the people of the prince that shall come shall destroy the city and the sanctuary,"** is talking about the **"prince"** who resided in Rome, during that time. In other words, this prophecy is predicting that sometime after 24 A.D., the army of the Roman Caesar (the prince in Rome) will destroy the city (Jerusalem), and the sanctuary (the temple).

Note: there are a few more things, that we need to discuss, before we continue with deciphering this prophecy.

Another reason, which explains why so many modern-day bible scholars fail to interpret the bible prophecies, correctly, is simply because some prophets will mention another prophecy, to help explain exactly when and how their new prophecy will be fulfilled. The **"desolations,"** mentioned in this prophecy, is the perfect example.

The **"desolations"** in this prophecy (Daniel 9:26), is referring to the fulfillment of another important prophecy, which was provided by Amos (Amos 8), who predicted that the **"desolations"** would begin to spread around the world, after the temple in Jerusalem, is destroyed:

> **"And the songs of the temple shall be howlings in that day, saith the Lord God: there shall be many dead bodies in every place; they shall cast them forth in silence"** (Amos 8:3).

When Amos mentions **"the songs of the temple,"** which **"shall be howlings in that day,"** and that **"there shall be many dead bodies in every place"** he was talking about the destruction of the temple, in Jerusalem. In the following scriptures, we learn that this is also when the **"famine of hearing the words of the Lord"** would begin (Amos 8:11-12).

> **"Behold, the days come, saith the Lord God, that I will send a famine in the land, not a famine of bread, nor a thirst for water, but of hearing the WORDS OF THE LORD: And they shall wander from sea to sea, and from the north even to the east, they shall run to and fro to seek the word of the Lord, and shall not find it"** (Amos 8:11-12).

Notice that Amos is talking about a **"famine,"** which would eventually spread around the world: not a famine of food, or water, but a famine of hearing the **"words of the Lord."** When Amos uses the phrase: **"the words of the Lord,"** he is talking about the gospel, and even predicts that there will be a time when this gospel will be lost. And even though many people, will search for this "lost gospel," they will not be able to find it: **"seek the word of the Lord, and shall not find it."**

The fact that Amos lived during the reign of Jeroboam II, who ruled over Israel approximately 200 years before Nebuchadnezzar was born, has caused many scholars to assume that Amos was talking about the first temple destruction, which occurred in 587 B.C. Understand; this prophecy was not overlooked by the bible scholars, but was simply placed in the unimportant file, because they knew that the temple destruction that occurred in 587 B.C., would not affect modern Christianity, today. The bible scholars understood that any gospel that was lost, in 587 B.C., would have been "restored," during the ministry of Jesus. However, this would be a completely different story, if the gospel was "lost," after the ministry of Jesus was completed. Even though their assumptions, concerning the first temple was correct, the bible scholars failed to recognize one very important detail. They failed to understand that the **"words of the Lord,"** did not exist, when Amos presented this prophecy. Therefore, it needs to be recognized that Amos was talking about the gospel that the Lord Jesus would teach, sometime in the distant future. This was the gospel that Amos was referring to as the **"words of the Lord."** This was the gospel that he warned would someday be lost and disappear from earth: **"And they shall wander from sea to sea, and from the north even to the east, they shall run to and fro to seek the word of the Lord, and shall not find it"** (Amos 8:11-12).

In other words, Amos was predicting that the true gospel of Jesus Christ would disappear, shortly after the temple in Jerusalem is destroyed, in 70 A.D.

This is the same event that Daniel (Daniel 9:26) was talking about, when he said: **"and the end thereof shall be with a flood, unto the end of the war desolations are determined."** In other words, shortly after the First Roman Jewish War is over, the **"desolations,"** which were previously **"determined"** (previously predicted by Amos), would begin to be fulfilled. Therefore, the true gospel that Jesus began teaching in 30 A.D., would disappear and be lost after the First Roman Jewish War is over in 70 A.D.

Even though Amos was talking about the temple in Jerusalem, it needs to be remembered that this temple was destroyed, twice: the first time happened, during the reign of Nebuchadnezzar in 587 B.C., while the second destruction was carried out by the Romans, in 70 A.D. In the following verse, Amos provides an accurate timetable, which will prove that Amos was talking about the second temple destruction, and not the first:

"They that swear by the sin of Samaria, and say, Thy god, O Dan, liveth; and, The manner of Beersheba liveth; even they shall fall, and never rise up again" (Amos 8:14).

At first glance, this verse does not appear to be very important, at all. However, after this verse is compared with the historical record, we discover that this verse is creating an accurate timetable, for exactly when the **"famine of hearing the words of the Lord"** would begin.

When studying the historical record, we learn that many of the ancient settlements, from Dan in the North to Beersheba in the South, were eventually rebuilt after Nebuchadnezzar attacked Israel, in 587 B.C. However, these ancient settlements were never rebuilt, after the Romans attacked Israel, in 70 A.D. This is because the Israelites were removed from their lands, which means that these ancient settlements remained uninhabited, from that time forward. This is what fulfilled the prophecy: **"even they shall fall, and never rise up again."**

When this verse mentions "Dan," it is referring to the "tribe of Dan," which became one of the lost tribes of Israel. When this verse says: **"They that swear by the sin of Samaria, and, The manner of Beersheba liveth,"** this is referring to the false religions, which were practiced within these ancient settlements. Even though the historical record proves that Samaria was rebuilt by the Romans, sometime during the second century, it needs to be remembered that this settlement was never rebuilt by any of the tribes of Israel. Therefore, when this prophecy predicted that the ancient settlements **"shall fall, and never rise up again,"** this prophecy is talking about the tribes of Israel, and how the different tribes would never rebuild these ancient settlements, after 70 A.D.

Note: this prophecy is talking about the ancient settlements of Israel, and Judah, and not talking about any modern cities that would exist, today. In fact, the ruins of these ancient settlements can still be seen, in modern times.

The ancient settlement at Beersheba, is the most important clue, which reveals exactly when this prophecy was fulfilled. Because Samaria, and the "tribe of Dan" were also mentioned, helped conceal this important timetable from the eyes of the world. The fact that Samaria is mentioned, and was later rebuilt by the Romans, added a little more confusion into the mix, which makes it appear that this prophecy was not fulfilled, at all. However, this prophecy was fulfilled, and the ancient settlements at Beersheba and Samaria were never rebuilt, by any of the tribes of Israel, after 70 A.D. The "tribe of Dan," also became one of the "ten lost tribes," which completely fulfilled the prophecy: **"even they shall fall, and never rise up again."**

Because verse fourteen (Amos 8:14) is talking about the second temple destruction, which occurred in 70 A.D., provides proof that Amos was talking about the true gospel that Jesus began teaching in 30 A.D. Therefore, the **"words of the Lord,"** which Amos predicted would disappear, and would not be found: **"And they shall wander from sea to sea, and from the north even to the east, they shall run to and fro to seek the word of the Lord, and shall not find it"** (Amos 8:11-12), is the true gospel that Jesus and his disciples taught: the "True Gospel of Jesus Christ."

Note: sometime later we will discuss a few more prophecies, which will reveal exactly when and how this "lost gospel" will be "restored," on earth.

But for now, we need to return to Daniel 9:26, to learn more about the desolations:

> **"And after threescore and two weeks shall Messiah be cut off, but not for himself: and the people of the prince that shall come shall destroy the city and the sanctuary; and the end thereof shall be with a flood, unto the end of the war DESOLATIONS are determined"** (Daniel 9:26).

When the bible uses the phrase **"desolation,"** it often means that the temple in Jerusalem, does not exist. Therefore, a new "desolation" period would begin, every time the temple in Jerusalem is destroyed. However, in Daniel's prophecies, we learn that the word **"desolations"** also has a double meaning. The **"desolations,"** which were predicted to happen **"after the war,"** is referring to the worldwide apostasy (a worldwide spiritual darkness), which Amos predicted would begin to spread around the world, after the **"words of the Lord"** are lost. His timetable (Amos 8:14) proves that his prophecy began to be fulfilled, shortly after the temple in Jerusalem was destroyed, in 70 A.D. The fact that the temple was destroyed, proves that another **"desolation"** period began, in 70 A.D.

The **"war"** mentioned: **"unto the end of the WAR desolations are determined"** (Daniel 9:26), is referring to the First Roman Jewish War, which began in 66 A.D. and ended in 70 A.D.

When Daniel's prophecy (Daniel 9:26) says: **"And AFTER threescore and two weeks,"** this is creating a timetable, for approximately when three different prophecies would be ready to be fulfilled. Notice that

DANIEL 9:26

the word **"after"** plays a very significant role in deciphering this prophecy. Therefore, sometime *after* a total of 434 years have passed (calculated from 457 B.C.), three different prophecies would then be ready to be fulfilled. In other words, none of these prophecies would begin to be fulfilled, until after 24 A.D. has passed.

Therefore, sometime *after* 24 A.D., Jesus would be killed: the temple in Jerusalem would be destroyed: and the "desolations" (the apostasy), predicted by Amos, would begin to spread around the world. See how simple? Nothing in this prophecy reveals exactly when any of these prophecies will be fulfilled. We are only informed, that none of these prophecies will be fulfilled, until sometime *after* 24 A.D. has passed.

Note: because most ministers often overlook the word **"after,"** should explain why so many ministers have failed, to solve this prophecy.

Because we successfully solved this prophecy (Daniel 9:26), we will now add the missing information, so we can fully understand what this prophecy is talking about:

"And after threescore and two weeks (after 434 years) **shall Messiah be cut off** (Messiah will be killed), **but not for himself** (for us): **and the people of the prince** (Caesar's Roman army) **that shall come shall destroy the city** (Jerusalem) **and the sanctuary** (the temple); **and the end thereof shall be with a flood** (of soldiers), **unto the end of the war desolations are determined,** and the apostasy, which was previously **"determined"** (previously predicted by Amos), will begin to spread around the world.

Note: the word apostasy, is referring to the spiritual darkness, which would cover the entire world, after the "True Gospel of Jesus Christ" is lost. The whole concept, concerning the "lost gospel," and how this "lost gospel" would affect modern Christianity, is completely misunderstood in modern times. Most ministers fail to understand that several bible prophecies predicted that the "True Gospel of Jesus Christ" would someday be lost. This is when the **"desolations"** (the apostasy) would begin to spread around the world. The prophecy in Daniel 9:26, concerning: **"and the end thereof shall be with a flood, unto the end of the war desolations are determined,"** will be discussed again, shortly, after we decipher Daniel 9:27:

Daniel 9:27

"And he shall confirm the covenant with many for one week: and in the midst of the week he shall cause the sacrifice and the oblation to cease, and for the overspreading of abominations he shall make it desolate, even until the consummation, and that determined shall be poured upon the desolate" (Daniel 9:27).

ONCE AGAIN, WE will divide this prophecy, in the following manner:

1. "And he shall confirm the covenant with many for one week"
2. "and in the midst of the week he shall cause the sacrifice and the oblation to cease"
3. "and for the overspreading of abominations he shall make it desolate, even until the consummation"
4. "and that determined shall be poured upon the desolate."

This prophecy predicts that four major events were scheduled to happen. When this verse says: **"And he shall confirm the covenant with many for one week,"** this is talking about the ministry of "John the Baptist," who would preach for a total of seven years (one week equals seven days). This verse then proclaims: **"and in the midst of the week,"** meaning in 3½ years, **"he shall cause the sacrifice and the oblation to cease."**

We need to be very careful, when deciphering this prophecy, because it would be a very serious error to assume that "John the Baptist" was the individual, who would **"cause the sacrifice and the oblation to cease."** This verse is talking about the priesthood duties, which "John the Baptist" performed, during his ministry. Therefore, this prophecy predicts that "John the Baptist" would perform a certain priesthood duty, which would eventually **"cause the sacrifice and the oblation to cease."** This is referring to the animal blood sacrifices, which were performed daily, for the oblation (or remission) of sins. The only individual who abolished this sacrificial law, and caused **"the sacrifice and oblation to cease,"** was none other than Jesus, himself. Therefore, this verse is simply letting us know that Jesus would arrive in Jerusalem, in the middle of John's ministry, in 3½ years from 27 A.D.

Notice that 3½ years from 27 A.D. is 30 A.D.

> 27 A.D. was the first year when "John the Baptist" began his ministry.
> 28 A.D. the second year
> 29 A.D. the third year
> 30 A.D. sometime after the sixth month: Jesus began his ministry.

This confirms what we previously discussed, after we studied the "Book of Luke," when Luke said that Jesus was baptized by "John the Baptist" in 30 A.D. (Luke 3:21-23). This confirms that Jesus began his ministry in 30 A.D.

Understand; the crucifixion of Jesus, permanently abolished the daily animal blood sacrifices, for the remission of sins: **"cause the sacrifice and oblation to cease."** Therefore, when "John the Baptist" began his ministry in 27 A.D., Jesus was scheduled to arrive in Jerusalem, in 30 A.D. Sometime later, Jesus would then be crucified, which is when the daily animal blood sacrifices for the remission of sins, would be permanently abolished.

The Desolations

We will now discuss the last prophecies in Daniel 9:26 and 27, and only concentrate on deciphering the last prophecy, in each verse:

Daniel 9:26: "And after threescore and two weeks shall Messiah be cut off, but not for himself: and the people of the prince that shall come shall destroy the city and the sanctuary; AND THE END THEREOF SHALL BE WITH A FLOOD, UNTO THE END OF THE WAR DESOLATIONS ARE DETERMINED."

When this verse says: **"and the end thereof shall be with a flood, unto the end of the war desolations are determined,"** this is talking about the First Roman Jewish War, which ended in 70 A.D. This is when the Romans attacked Jerusalem with a **"flood"** of soldiers. After this war was over: **"unto the end of the war"** another prophecy, concerning the **"desolations are determined,"** began to be fulfilled. This is referring to the **"desolations"** (the apostasy), which Amos predicted (**"determined"**) would begin to spread around the world, after 70 A.D. Therefore, after the Romans attacked Jerusalem with a "flood" of soldiers, the temple was destroyed, and this is when the prophecy of Amos (Amos 8) began to be fulfilled, and the **"words of the Lord"** were lost: referring to the "True Gospel of Jesus Christ."

This is explained, again, in verse twenty-seven:

Daniel 9:27: "And he shall confirm the covenant with many for one week: and in the midst of the week he shall cause the sacrifice and the oblation to cease, AND FOR THE OVERSPREADING OF ABOMINATIONS HE SHALL MAKE IT DESOLATE, EVEN UNTIL THE CONSUMMATION, AND THAT DETERMINED SHALL BE POURED UPON THE DESOLATE."

The last part of this prophecy, which says: **"and for the overspreading of abominations he shall make it desolate, even until the consummation, and that determined shall be poured upon the desolate"** confirms what we previously discussed. In other words, the people in Jerusalem, Israel, and Judah caused a great apostasy (**"the overspreading of abominations"**) to spread around the world, because the people in Israel turned their backs on Jesus, and the gospel that he taught. Because of this evil transgression, these people received a great punishment from God, and this is when the temple in Jerusalem was destroyed: **"he shall make it desolate."** This is when the land of Israel also became **"desolate."** Shortly after this prophecy was fulfilled (**"consummated"**), another prophecy, which was predicted by Amos (**"determined"** by Amos), began to be fulfilled. This is when the apostasy (predicted by Amos) began to spread around the world, which was poured upon the desolate: **"shall be poured upon the desolate."** This **"desolation,"** was poured **"upon the desolate"** people, because the "True Gospel of Jesus Christ" was lost.

In the following verse, Jeremiah explains why the temple in Jerusalem, was destroyed, in 587 B.C. Notice that this is the same reason why the temple was destroyed, again, in 70 A.D.

"So that the Lord could no longer bear, because of the evil of

your doings, and because of the ABOMINATIONS which ye have committed; therefore is your land a DESOLATION, and an astonishment, and a curse, without an inhabitant, as at this day"** (Jeremiah 44:22).

We find the word **"desolate"** mentioned several times in the "Book of Psalms." Notice that this word was also applied to individuals:

"Turn thee unto me, and have mercy upon me; for I am DESOLATE and afflicted" (Psalms 25:16).

"Evil shall slay the wicked: and they that hate the righteous shall be DESOLATE" (Psalms 34:21).

"The Lord redeemeth the soul of his servants: and none of them that trust in him shall be DESOLATE" (Psalms 34:22).

"Therefore is my spirit overwhelmed within me; my heart within me is DESOLATE" (Psalms 143:4).

The word "desolate," in these examples, prove that the people living in this "desolate" condition, would be living their lives in "spiritual darkness," which could eventually cause them to be completely separated from God.

In accordance with Daniel's prophecies, this "spiritual darkness" was scheduled to be **"poured"** upon the **"desolate"** people, shortly after 70 A.D. According to Amos, this began to happen as soon as the "True Gospel of Jesus Christ" was lost:

"Behold, the days come, saith the Lord God, that I will send a famine in the land, not a famine of bread, nor a thirst for water, but of hearing the WORDS OF THE LORD: And

they shall wander from sea to sea, and from the north even to the east, they shall run to and fro to seek the word of the Lord, and shall not find it" (Amos 8:11-12).

The fact that we now have the Holy Bible in our possession, today, will cause many Christians to question this whole concept. However, it needs to be remembered that these prophecies were written in the Holy Bible. Therefore, we learn from studying the bible scriptures (Daniel 9:26-27), that the prophecy of Amos would be fulfilled, shortly after 70 A.D. We also learn from the bible scriptures, that the "True Gospel of Jesus Christ" (**"the words of the Lord"**), would someday be lost. Why would the bible scriptures tell us that the "True Gospel of Jesus Christ" would be lost, and not be found, if the Holy Bible contains the "True Gospel of Jesus Christ?" For that matter: why does the Holy Bible talk about the "restoration" prophecies, which predict that the "True Gospel of Jesus Christ" will be "restored," on earth, during the "last days?" Why do any of these prophecies exist, if everything that we would ever need to know, is found in the Holy Bible?

Here is a short review, for what we learned, from Daniel's prophecies:

1. "John the Baptist" would begin his seven-year ministry in 27 A.D.
2. In the middle of John's ministry, in 3½ years (30 A.D.), Jesus would arrive in Jerusalem to begin his ministry, which began shortly after he was baptized by "John the Baptist" (Luke 3:21-23).
3. Sometime later, Jesus was killed (crucified for us), and through his physical blood sacrifice, the daily animal blood sacrifices for the **oblation** (remission) of sins were abolished: **"he shall cause the sacrifice and the oblation to cease."**
4. After these prophecies are fulfilled, Jerusalem, Israel, and Judah were attacked by a **"flood"** of Roman soldiers. This is

when the temple in Jerusalem was destroyed, and the land became **"desolate"** ("spiritually desolate"), from that time forward.

5. This is when the apostasy, which Amos predicted would happen (**"and that determined"**), began to spread around the world. This spiritual darkness was also poured upon the **"desolate"** people: **"shall be poured upon the desolate."**

6. In accordance with the prophecy of Amos, this happened as soon as the **"words of the Lord"** (the "True Gospel of Jesus Christ") was lost, shortly after 70 A.D. This is when the prophecy of Amos: **"they shall wander from sea to sea, and from the north even to the east, they shall run to and fro to seek the word of the Lord, and shall not find it"** (Amos 8:11-12), was fulfilled.

The Seventy Weeks in Daniel 9:24

With these prophecies solved, we will now go back, and decipher verse twenty-four. Understand; this prophecy could not be deciphered earlier, simply because we did not have an accurate date, to begin our calculations. Many ministers have failed to solve this prophecy, because they do not understand that this verse is out of order, which means that this prophecy is the last prophecy in this series. We will now continue:

> **Daniel 9:24: "SEVENTY WEEKS are determined upon thy people and upon thy holy city, to finish the transgression, and to make an end of sins, and to make reconciliation for iniquity, and to bring in everlasting righteousness, and to seal up the vision and prophecy, and to anoint the most holy."**

We learn from this prophecy that something important was scheduled to happen, in 70 weeks, calculated as follows: 70 weeks, times 7 days, equals 490 days: meaning 490 years. The most important thing to remember, concerning this prophecy, is the fact that the people in Jerusalem (**"thy holy city"**) were given a total of seventy weeks (490 years) to: **"MAKE AND END OF SINS"** and to **"ANOINT THE**

MOST HOLY." This prophecy is calculated from the time that the **"edict to restore"** document was officially placed in force. Therefore, this prophecy is simply letting us know that in 490 years, from 457 B.C., a very important event was scheduled to happen, in Jerusalem. This event would **"make an end of sins"** and **"anoint the most holy."** The event that was scheduled to happen, in 490 years from 457 B.C., was the crucifixion of Jesus. As a result, it would be through his physical blood sacrifice, which would cleanse the people from their sins: **"make an end of sins,"** and would **"anoint"** Jesus Christ, as the **"most holy."**

Therefore, when we calculate forward 490 years from 457 B.C., we end up with 33, and when we add the one missing zero-year, we end up with 34 A.D. In other words, the mathematics in this prophecy has just proven that Jesus was crucified, in 34 A.D.

Note: the actual year for when Jesus was crucified is rather controversial, in modern times, because many modern-day bible scholars have different theories, concerning what year Jesus was crucified.

Question: is there any proof that 34 A.D. is accurate?

This is where the following prophecy comes into play.

Daniel 12:11-12

This is another prophecy, which is completely misunderstood by most modern-day bible scholars, today. This prophecy was provided by Daniel, to prove that every mathematical calculation that we performed, were completely accurate and true:

> "And from the time that the daily sacrifice shall be taken away, and the abomination that maketh desolate set up, there shall be a thousand two hundred and ninety days. blessed is he that waiteth, and cometh to the thousand three hundred and five and thirty days" (Daniel 12:11-12).

We will now separate this prophecy in the following manner:

1. "And from the time that the daily sacrifice shall be taken away,
2. and the abomination that maketh desolate set up,
3. there shall be a thousand two hundred and ninety days.
4. blessed is he that waiteth, and cometh to the thousand three hundred and five and thirty days"

The first thing to remember, is that the crucifixion of Jesus permanently abolished the daily animal blood sacrifices, for the remission of sins. Therefore, it was the crucifixion of Jesus, which is being referred to in this prophecy, as: **"And from the time that the daily sacrifice shall be taken away."** This is the year that we will now use to solve this prophecy. Understand; it would not be possible to solve this prophecy, if we used the wrong year, to begin our calculations.

Therefore, **"And from the time that the daily sacrifice shall be taken away"** in 34 A.D., to when **"the abomination that maketh desolate"** will be **"set up,"** will be a total of 1290 days (years). This means that **"the abomination that maketh desolate,"** will be **"set up,"** in 1324 A.D.

We are then informed that another prophecy: **"Blessed is he that waiteth,"** will *begin* to be fulfilled, 1335 years from 34 A.D. Understand; this scripture is not saying that this prophecy will be completely fulfilled, in 1335 years, but only predicts that sometime in 1369 A.D., this prophecy will *begin* to be fulfilled.

As you can see, it would not be possible to find the secret hidden messages, if we used the wrong year to begin these calculations.

This prophecy is simply predicting the birth of two very important men in Christian history:

John Wycliffe was born in **1324 A.D.**
John Huss was born in **1369 A.D.**

This prophecy not only proves that 457 B.C. was the correct year to begin our calculations, but it also proves that 34 A.D. was the correct year, for when Jesus was crucified. This also proves that "John the Baptist" began his seven-year ministry, in 27 A.D., and that Jesus began his ministry in 30 A.D. The fact that Jesus was 30 years old, in 30 A.D., also proves that Jesus was born in 1 B.C. Therefore, this prophecy confirms that every mathematical calculation that we performed, were completely accurate and true. This prophecy also proves that God knows all things, before they happen, and that Daniel was a true prophet of God.

The **"set up"** is talking about how the world stage, would be **"set up,"** which would allow **"the abomination that maketh desolate"** possible. It needs to be understood that this prophecy is not predicting that **"the abomination that maketh desolate"** will be fulfilled, in 1324 A.D., but only predicts that the world stage will be **"set up,"** which would then allow **"the abomination that maketh desolate"** to be fulfilled, sometime after 1324 A.D.

To understand what role John Wycliffe played, in setting up the world stage (the **"set up"),** for **"the abomination that maketh desolate,"** requires that we fully understand that the different Christian churches, disagree on a wide range of religious issues. These churches cannot even agree, concerning how the bible scriptures should be interpreted, and taught. Many years before John Wycliffe was born, the Catholic Church was the only source for the false interpretations, and false doctrines that existed. This is because the Catholic Church controlled everything that was taught in the Christian world. However, this gradually began to change after John Wycliffe arrived on the scene, because he not only translated the Holy Bible into the English language, but he also wrote extensively about Christianity, and what he envisioned Christianity should be. As a result, many people began to formulate their personal religious beliefs, based upon what John Wycliffe and his ministers taught. In other words, this is when many new and different Christian theories, and doctrines were introduced, into the Christian community. In accordance with Daniel's prophecy, it was John Wycliffe who **"set up"** the world stage, which would allow many more false doctrines, and false interpretations to be taught throughout the Christian world. When Daniel talks about **"the abomination that maketh desolate,"** he was talking about the false Christian doctrines, and false interpretations, which would eventually spread around the world. Because these false Christian doctrines are an **"abomination,"** against the "word of God," these false doctrines will lead many Christians into the dark world of spiritual **"desolation."** This explains why these false Christian doctrines are referred to as: **"the abomination that maketh desolate."**

Several years later, John Huss discovered some of John Wycliffe's writings, and began to study what he wrote. This is when John Huss realized that the official authority of the church, remained in the hands of Jesus, because Jesus was the "rock." John Huss was talking about the authority of the Catholic Church, and how this church misinterpreted, the following scriptures:

> "When Jesus came into the coasts of Caesarea Philippi, he asked his disciples, saying, Whom do men say that I the Son of man am? And they said, Some say that thou art John the Baptist: some, Elias; and others, Jeremias, or one of the prophets. He saith unto them, But whom say ye that I am? And Simon Peter answered and said, Thou art the Christ, the Son of the living God. And Jesus answered and said unto him, Blessed art thou, Simon Bar-jona: for flesh and blood hath not revealed it unto thee, but my Father which is in heaven. And I say also unto thee, That thou art Peter, AND UPON THIS ROCK I WILL BUILD MY CHURCH; and the gates of hell shall not prevail against it. And I will give unto thee the keys of the kingdom of heaven: and whatsoever thou shalt bind on earth shall be bound in heaven: and whatsoever thou shalt loose on earth shall be loosed in heaven" (Matthew 16:13-19).

Because the Catholic Church misinterpreted the phrase: **"That thou art Peter, and upon this rock I will build my church,"** and also misinterpreted: **"And I will give unto thee the keys of the kingdom of heaven,"** the church assumed that Jesus gave Peter the authority to build God's church, on earth. However, when John Huss recognized that Jesus was the "rock," he then began to understand that Jesus was simply confirming to Peter, what Peter already knew: that Jesus was the "rock," who would build his church, on earth: the Church of Jesus Christ. When Jesus replied to Peter: **"and upon this rock I will build my church,"** and then said: **"And I will give unto thee the keys of the kingdom of heaven,"** this was just another way for Jesus to explain to Peter, that he would soon receive the authority of the Holy Priesthood. In other words, the **"keys of the kingdom of heaven,"** is referring to the authority of the Holy Priesthood, which has the power to "seal" and to "unseal," explained as: **"and whatsoever thou shalt bind on earth shall be bound in heaven: and whatsoever thou shalt loose on earth shall be loosed in heaven."** The priesthood holders must first receive these "keys," before officially performing any holy ordinance on earth, which will then be accepted in heaven. Therefore, it would not be possible to perform any holy ordinance on earth, and have it officially accepted in heaven, without these **"keys."** How these different **"keys"** are received, and how they are distributed among the various priesthood holders, is another thing that most modern-day ministers do not understand.

In either case, it needs to be understood that the entire foundation for the Catholic Church, is based upon how this church interprets these scriptures. To have someone like John Huss question the authority of the Catholic Church, and then accuse them of misinterpreting the scriptures, was unforgiveable. Therefore, because this was a very serious offense against the Catholic Church, itself, caused John Huss to be charged with heresy. He was then burned at the stake on July

16, 1415. This was the event that fulfilled the prophecy: **"blessed is he that waiteth."** In other words, the fact that John Huss was put to death, because he was defending his faith in Jesus, caused him to be **"blessed"** forever.

Daniel 12:4 and the "Restoration"

Earlier, when we talked about the prophecy of Amos, we discovered that the **"words of the Lord"** would be lost, and not be found:

> **"Behold, the days come, saith the Lord God, that I will send a famine in the land, not a famine of bread, nor a thirst for water, but of hearing the WORDS OF THE LORD: And they shall wander from sea to sea, and from the north even to the east, they shall run to and fro to seek the word of the Lord, and shall not find it"** (Amos 8:11-12).

In the next prophecy, we discover that the exact opposite thing will happen, during the last days, because this is when knowledge (about God) will increase:

> **"But thou, O Daniel, shut up the words, and seal the book, even to the time of the end: many shall run to and fro, AND KNOWLEDGE SHALL BE INCREASED"** (Daniel 12:4).

The first prophecy (Amos 8:11-12) was fulfilled shortly after 70 A.D., while Daniel's prophecy (Daniel 12:4) was not scheduled to be fulfilled, until sometime during the "last days." This is when the "restoration" prophecies were scheduled to be fulfilled, and when knowledge about God, would increase.

One "restoration" prophecy reads as follows:

> **"And he shall send Jesus Christ, which before was preached unto you: Whom the heaven must receive UNTIL the times of restitution of all things, which God hath spoken by the mouth of all his holy prophets since the world began"** (Acts 3:20-21).

In accordance with this prophecy, we learn that there will be a time when a **"restitution of all things"** will happen, on earth. Notice that this will happen sometime *before* Jesus returns, because we are also told that Jesus will remain in heaven: **"Whom the heaven must receive,"** **until** it is time for the **"restitution of all things"** prophecy to be fulfilled: **"the times of restitution of all things."**

In the next prophecy we learn exactly when this will happen:

> **"That in the DISPENSATION OF THE FULNESS OF TIMES he might gather together in one all things in Christ, both which are in heaven, and which are on earth; even in him"** (Ephesians 1:10).

Therefore, we learn that the **"restitution of all things"** prophecy will be fulfilled, sometime during **"the dispensation of the fulness of times."**

Question: what exactly is a **"dispensation,"** and how many dispensations have we had, in the past?

We could say that there was a dispensation of Adam and Eve; a dispensation of Moses; a dispensation of Abraham; a dispensation of "John the Baptist;" and a dispensation of Jesus. In this prophecy, we are now being told that there will be another dispensation, which is referred to as **"the dispensation of the fulness of times,"** when many things will be "restored" on earth: this period is also referred to as the **"restitution of all things."**

From the prophecies of Amos (Amos 8) and Daniel (Daniel 9:26-27), we discovered that **"the desolation"** began to spread, around the world, shortly after 70 A.D. When you combine the "spiritual darkness," with the various disagreements that exist within the Christian churches, today, you begin to recognize that the entire Christian community is in some serious trouble. The fact that these disagreements exist, in the first place, and affects every Christian in the modern Christian world, should explain why the "restoration" (**"restitution of all things"**) would be needed. During this "restitution" period is when the "True Gospel of Jesus Christ" was also scheduled to be "restored" on earth.

Question: why would we need a **"restitution of all things,"** if nothing is missing, from the bible scriptures?

For that matter, what is missing from the bible scriptures, which is so important that we would need a **"restitution of all things"** to "restore" this missing information, on earth?

Understand; the Holy Bible was compiled together, sometime during the third and fourth centuries, which was long after the ministry of Jesus was completed. Even though the bible scriptures have been thoroughly examined, throughout its existence, most bible scholars cannot explain why a "restoration" (or a "restitution") would be needed. From their point of view, they often profess that everything that we will ever need to know, is in the bible. Obviously, they do not understand the "restoration" prophecies, or the fact that the "Holy Bible" predicted that the "True Gospel of Jesus Christ" would eventually be "restored" on earth.

The correct terminology, for this "spiritual darkness," is referred to as the "apostasy." Therefore, when the bible speaks about the "apostasy," it will often use words like "darkness," or "spiritual darkness," or "gross darkness." This is referring to the fact that when you move away from the "spiritual light," or the "light of God," you begin to enter the dark world filled with "spiritual darkness." The phrase, "worldwide apostasy," is referring to the fact that this "spiritual darkness" would eventually cover the entire world.

When the bible speaks about the people in apostasy, they are often referred to as "sleeping," or "their eyes are closed," or "they cannot see or hear," or they are "blind." In some cases, the bible will also use words like "staggering," and "drunkenness." In either case, it needs to be understood that the darkest time, on earth, would exist during the time when the apostasy covers the entire world. This would be the darkest time, simply because nothing would exist anywhere on earth, which could save mankind from this fallen condition. During a complete worldwide apostasy, is when **all knowledge** about God, would completely disappear. However, God decided that mankind should never reach this extreme level of "spiritual darkness." Therefore, to stop this from happening, the Holy Bible was created, so people could learn something about God, and Jesus Christ, long after Israel, Judah, and Jerusalem were destroyed.

Daniel 11:32-34 and the Holy Bible

"And such as do wickedly against the covenant shall he corrupt by flatteries: but the people that do know their God shall be strong, and do exploits. And they that understand among the people shall instruct many: yet they shall fall by the sword, and by flame, by captivity, and by spoil, many days. Now when they shall fall, they shall be holpen with a LITTLE HELP: but many shall cleave to them with flatteries" (Daniel 11:32-34).

These scriptures are explaining what happened, after 70 A.D., after the Romans destroyed Jerusalem. Notice that the people who taught the "True Gospel of Jesus Christ," to others, after 70 A.D., were eventually killed. This is when the "True Gospel of Jesus Christ" was lost, and when the **"famine of hearing the words of the Lord"** began to spread, around the world. Several centuries later, God decided to send a **"little help,"** which arrived on scene as the Holy Bible. However, in accordance with these scriptures, we were also warned that many people would use the bible scriptures for personal gain, and would tell people what they wanted to hear, rather than the truth: **"but many**

shall cleave to them with flatteries." When the phrase **"little help"** was used, in this prophecy, this meant that the Holy Bible was scheduled to arrive on earth, by itself. Therefore, a true prophet of God was not sent, to teach the people the correct interpretation of the scriptures. Because this important help was not sent, explains why the bible scriptures continue to be misinterpreted, today, and why so many ministers use the bible scriptures, for personal gain: **"but many shall cleave to them with flatteries"**

Isaiah 60:1-3 and "Thy Light"

"Arise, shine; for thy light is come, and the glory of the Lord is risen upon thee. For, behold, the darkness shall cover the earth, and gross darkness the people: but the Lord shall arise upon thee, and his glory shall be seen upon thee. And the Gentiles shall come to thy light, and kings to the brightness of thy rising" (Isaiah 60:1-3).

When Isaiah proclaims:

"For, behold, the darkness shall cover the earth, and gross darkness the people," he is also talking about the worldwide spiritual darkness (the apostasy), which would eventually cover the entire world. He then proclaims: **"but the Lord shall arise upon thee, and his glory shall be seen upon thee,"** which he predicts would happen, after the prophecy: **"And the Gentiles shall come to thy light, and kings to the brightness of thy rising"** is fulfilled.

This prophecy is the perfect example, which demonstrates how a secret message can be delivered, and at the same time, remain hid from the eyes of the world. This secret message is letting us know, that at some point **"the Gentiles shall come to thy light,"** which also means that

the **"Gentiles"** will receive the "True Gospel of Jesus Christ." The fact that "spiritual light" has the power to remove the "spiritual darkness," also proves that when the Gentiles **"come to thy light,"** that this event will begin to remove the apostasy from earth. Isaiah then provides an accurate timetable, for exactly when this event was scheduled to happen, when he uses the phrase: **"kings to the brightness of thy rising."** This secret message is referring to another prophecy, which Daniel provided, many years later:

> **"And IN THE DAYS OF THESE KINGS shall the God of heaven set up a kingdom, which shall never be destroyed: and the kingdom shall not be left to other people, but it shall break in pieces and consume all these kingdoms, and it shall stand forever,"** (Daniel 2:44).

Therefore, Isaiah was simply letting us know that sometime in the distant future (from his perspective), the Gentiles will receive **"thy light"** (the "True Gospel of Jesus Christ"), during the time when Daniel's prophecy: **"in the days of these kings"** is fulfilled. Also notice that Daniel's prophecy, also predicts that sometime during **"the days of these kings,"** is when the "Kingdom of God" (God's True Church) will be established, on earth. Therefore, after the **"Gentiles shall come to thy light,"** and after the "Kingdom of God" is established on earth, the "spiritual darkness" (the apostasy) will begin to be removed from earth.

Isaiah's prophecy, concerning **"the Gentiles shall come to thy light,"** is another prophecy that many ministers have failed to understand. One reason is because the timetable, which Isaiah provides, remains hid from the eyes of the world. Therefore, when most modern-day ministers teach their congregations about Isaiah's prophecy, concerning **"the Gentiles shall come to thy light"** (Isaiah 60:3), many ministers assume that Isaiah was talking about the ministry of Jesus. Therefore, they contend that sometime during the ministry of Jesus, the Gentiles would receive **"thy light."** Even though the Gentiles did receive **"thy light,"** for the first time, during the ministry of Jesus: **"Arise, shine; for thy light is come, and the glory of the Lord is risen upon thee,"** the Gentiles were also scheduled to receive **"thy light"** for a second time, many centuries later. This event was scheduled to happen, during the **"days of these kings,"** just like Daniel predicted (Daniel 2:44).

To fully understand what Isaiah was talking about, requires that we separate his scripture (Isaiah 60:1-3), in the following manner:

1. **Arise, shine; for thy light is come, and the glory of the Lord is risen upon thee.**
2. **For, behold, the darkness shall cover the earth, and gross darkness the people:**
3. **but the Lord shall arise upon thee, and his glory shall be seen upon thee.**
4. **And the Gentiles shall come to thy light, and kings to the brightness of thy rising"**

In the first sentence we are told:

"Arise, shine; for thy light is come, and the glory of the Lord is risen upon thee" (Isaiah 60:1).

When Isaiah uses the phrase **"for thy light is come, and the glory of the Lord is risen upon thee,"** he is talking about what happened to the Gentiles, during the ministry of Jesus (Luke 2:32; Acts 9:15; 1 Timothy 2:7; 3:16; Galatians 3:14). This is when the Gentiles received **"thy light"** for the first time.

When this prophecy says: **"For, behold, the darkness shall cover the earth, and gross darkness the people,"** Isaiah was talking about what happened, **after** the ministry of Jesus was completed, when the spiritual darkness (the apostasy) began to cover the entire world. Sometime later, after the apostasy covers the entire world, is when another prophecy: **"but the Lord shall arise upon thee, and his glory shall be seen upon thee"** will be fulfilled. This was scheduled to happen when the prophecy: **"and kings to the brightness of thy rising,"** is fulfilled, which is referring to the prophecy that Daniel provided (Daniel 2:44):

"And IN THE DAYS OF THESE KINGS shall the God of heaven set up a kingdom, which shall never be destroyed: and the kingdom shall not be left to other people, but it shall break in pieces and consume all these kingdoms, and it shall stand forever," (Daniel 2:44).

Here is how, the prophecies of Daniel and Isaiah, are directly connected:

1. During the ministry of Jesus, the Gentiles received **"thy light,"** for the first time.
2. After the temple in Jerusalem was destroyed, in 70 A.D., **"the words of the Lord"** (the "True Gospel of Jesus Christ") disappeared from earth, which fulfilled the prophecy of Amos, concerning the **"famine of hearing the words of the Lord."** This is when the **"abomination of desolation,"** and the "spiritual darkness" (the apostasy), began to spread around the world.
3. Many centuries later, after **"the darkness shall cover the earth, and gross darkness the people,"** the Gentiles would then receive **"thy light,"** for a second time. This was scheduled to happen, sometime during the "latter-days," after Daniel's "ten kings" prophecy is fulfilled: referred to in Isaiah's prophecy as: **"and kings to the brightness of thy rising."**
4. When Daniel's prophecy (Daniel 2:44) is fulfilled, during the reign of the "kings," is when the "Kingdom of God" (God's True Church) will be established, on earth.

It needs to be remembered that when Daniel talks about the "Kingdom of God," he is talking about God's True Church, which was scheduled to be established on earth, during the **"days of these kings"** (Daniel 2:44). This is where Daniel's "Ten Kings" prophecy comes into play.

Daniel's "Ten Kings"

WHEN WE STUDY Nebuchadnezzar's dream (Daniel 2:31-44), we learn about several different kingdoms, which were scheduled to come to power.

Here is Nebuchadnezzar's dream, as written, in the "King James Version:"

> Daniel 2:31, "Thou O King, sawest, and behold a great image. This great image, whose brightness was excellent, stood before thee: and the form thereof was terrible."

> Daniel 2:32, "This image's head was of fine gold, his breast and his arms of silver, his belly and his thighs of brass."

> Daniel 2:33, "His legs of iron, his feet part of iron and part of clay."

> Daniel 2:34, "Thou sawest till that a stone was cut out without hands, which smote the image upon his feet that were of iron and clay, and brake them to pieces."

> Daniel 2:35, "Then was the iron, the clay, the brass, the

> silver, and the gold, broken to pieces together, and became like the chaff of the summer threshing floors; and the wind carried them, that no place was found for them: and the stone that smote the image became a great mountain, and filled the whole earth."

Here is what we need to know before we attempt to decipher this prophecy:

> The first kingdom, represented by gold, is the "Babylonian Empire."
>
> The second kingdom, represented by silver, is the "Great Persian Empire."
>
> The third kingdom, represented by brass, is the "Macedonian-Greek Empire."
>
> The fourth kingdom, represented by the two legs of iron, is the "Roman Republic, which would eventually evolve into the "Holy Roman Empire."

These four kingdoms were also represented by four powerful beasts:

> The Lion represents the "Babylonian Empire."
>
> The Bear represents the "Great Persian Empire."
>
> The Leopard represents the "Macedonian-Greek Empire."
>
> The "great and terrible beast, with its iron teeth and ten horns," represents the "Roman Republic" and the "Holy Roman Empire."

Daniel 2:38-43

We learn from Nebuchadnezzar's dream, that there would also be a fifth kingdom, made **"part of iron, and part of clay:"**

> **Daniel 2:42, "and as the toes of the feet were part of iron, and part of clay, so the kingdom shall be partly strong, and partly broken."**

> **Daniel 2:43, "and whereas thou sawest iron mixed with miry clay, they shall mingle themselves with the seed of men: but they shall not cleave one to another, even as iron is not mixed with clay."**

And then sometime later, during the reign of this fifth kingdom, is when a sixth kingdom ("Kingdom of God") will be established, on earth:

> **Daniel 2:44, "And in the days of these kings shall the God of heaven set up a kingdom, which shall never be destroyed: and the kingdom shall not be left to other people, but it shall break in pieces and consume all these kingdoms, and it shall stand forever."**

Note: many bible scholars misunderstand the role that the fourth kingdom would play, during the reign of the fifth kingdom, made of clay. As a result, they fail to identify this fifth kingdom, and what role the "ten kings" played, in fulfilling this prophecy. They also fail to understand the terminology, concerning the "Kingdom of God," and how this prophecy was scheduled to be fulfilled, on earth, before Jesus returns. As a result, many ministers teach their congregations that the "Kingdom of God," in Daniel's prophecy, is talking about the "Kingdom of God," which would be established on earth, after Jesus returns. What these ministers fail to understand, concerns the fact that the "Kingdom of God" is just another name for God's True Church, which would be established on earth, during the "latter-days," **before** Jesus returns. In accordance with Daniel's prophecy (Daniel 2:44), this was scheduled to happen, during the reign of the fifth kingdom with its "ten kings," as predicted in Nebuchadnezzar's dream.

Daniel 7:3-7

At first glance, these different beasts appear to be rather scary, but the scary elements completely disappear, after people learn that these four beasts represent four powerful kingdoms:

> "And FOUR great beasts came up from the sea, diverse one from another. The first was like a LION, and had eagle's wings: I beheld till the wings thereof were plucked, and it was lifted up from the earth, and made stand upon the feet as a man, and a man's heart was given to it. And behold another beast, a second, like to a BEAR, and it raised up itself on one side, and it had three ribs in the mouth of it between the teeth of it: and they said thus unto it, Arise, devour much flesh. After this I beheld, and lo another, like a LEOPARD, which had upon the back of it four wings of a fowl; the beast had also four heads; and dominion was given to it. After this I saw in the night visions, and behold a FOURTH BEAST, DREADFUL AND TERRIBLE, AND STRONG EXCEEDINGLY; and it had great iron teeth: it devoured and brake in pieces, and stamped the residue with the feet of it: and it was diverse from all the beasts that were before it; AND IT HAD TEN HORNS" (Daniel 7:3-7).

Here is how this prophecy should be deciphered:

> **"The first was like a LION, and had eagle's wings: I beheld till the WINGS thereof were plucked, and it was lifted up from the earth, and made stand upon the feet as a man, and a man's heart was given to it"** (Daniel 7:4).

The LION represents the "Babylonian Empire," while the WINGS represent the power of this kingdom, and how this kingdom lost its power, after King Nebuchadnezzar died: for this is when **"the wings thereof were plucked,"** and the power of the "Babylonian Empire," was greatly diminished. In comparison, if we plucked the feathers from the wings of a bird, the power of the bird would be greatly diminished, simply because it would not be able to fly, or even defend itself. The king who succeeded Nebuchadnezzar, was Nabonidus (the father of Belshazzar), who did not establish any personal relationship with God, which means that he ruled over his kingdom with a **"man's heart."** The fact that this verse also proclaims: **"and made stand upon the feet as a man, and a man's heart was given to it,** simply means that this king was forced to stand on his own feet, because he would not receive any help or protection from God. Therefore, the destiny of the "Babylonian Empire," was left in the hands of this king.

> **"And behold another beast, a second, like to a BEAR, and it raised up itself on one side, and it had three ribs in the mouth of it between the teeth of it: and they said thus unto it, Arise, devour much flesh"** (Daniel 7:5).

The BEAR represents the "Great Persian Empire," which was governed by two separate kings, who ruled over this kingdom together: a Mede and a Persian. This division in leadership explains why we see the bear out of balance: **"and it raised up itself on one side."** This bear is out of balance because the power of this kingdom was also out of balance.

The three ribs, in the mouth of the bear, represent the three continents that the "Great Persian Empire" once occupied: part of Europe; part of Asia; and part of Africa.

"After this I beheld, and lo another, like a LEOPARD, which had upon the back of it four wings of a fowl; the beast had also four heads; and dominion was given to it" (Daniel 7:6).

The LEOPARD with its four wings and four heads, represent the "Macedonian-Greek Empire," governed by "Alexander the Great," which was divided among his powerful generals, after his death. After this kingdom was divided, it eventually evolved into four powerful dynasties: the Antigonid Dynasty, the Ptolemaic Dynasty, the Seleucid Dynasty, and the Attalid Dynasty. When this verse says: **"and dominion was given to it,"** this simply means that after this kingdom was divided up, it would still have the power to conquer many other kingdoms.

"After this I saw in the night visions, and behold a FOURTH BEAST, DREADFUL AND TERRIBLE, AND STRONG EXCEEDINGLY; and it had great iron teeth: it devoured and brake in pieces, and stamped the residue with the feet of it: and it was diverse from all the beasts that were before it; AND IT HAD TEN HORNS" (Daniel 7:7).

This FOURTH BEAST represents the "Roman Republic," the "Roman Empire," the "Holy Roman Empire," and the "Holy Roman Empire of the German Nation." The "ten horns" represent the ten kings, who once ruled from within the "Holy Roman Empire of the German Nation," as the "League of the Rhine." This fourth kingdom was **"diverse from all the beasts that were before it,"** simply because it ruled over a vast amount of territory, which included many different races, languages, and cultures.

It needs to be understood that Daniel does not separate the Roman Republic, from the "Holy Roman Empire," or the "Holy Roman Empire of the German Nation" when he talks about this fourth kingdom. Therefore, this fourth kingdom immediately took its turn in power, as soon as it defeated Macedonia in battle. There are many historians who contend that Charlemagne was the first "Holy Roman Emperor," after he was crowned by the Pope, in 800 A.D. There are others who contend that the first "Holy Roman Emperor," was "Otto the Great," after he was crowned in 962. In either case, because we are studying Daniel's prophecies, we must approach his prophecies from his perspective. Therefore, in accordance with Daniel's prophecies, as soon as Augustus Caesar (Octavius) received his religious title of "Augustus" (meaning: "the exalted one"), this is when he became the first ruler of the "Holy Roman Empire." It was this religious connection, to the false gods, which made the "Holy Roman Empire" so dangerous to Christians. Even though many modern-day historians would disagree with Daniel, concerning Augustus Caesar, the fact remains that the German Nation still recognizes that Augustus Caesar was the first leader, of the First Reich (or first kingdom).

Here is a list of these kingdoms, in order, and when they ruled:

1. **The first kingdom is the Babylonian Empire, represented by the head of Gold, and the Lion with eagle's wings** *(ruled from 608 B.C. to 538 B.C.)*.
2. **The second kingdom is the "Great Persian Empire," represented by the breast and arms of silver, and the Bear,** *(this kingdom conquered Babylon in 538 B.C. and remained in power until 330 B.C.)*.
3. **The third kingdom is the Macedonian-Greek Empire, represented by the belly and thighs of brass, and the Leopard with its four wings and four heads** *(this kingdom conquered*

the Persian Empire in 330 B.C., and remained in power until Macedonia became a Roman state, in 149 B.C.).

4. **The fourth kingdom is the Roman Empire, represented by the legs of iron, and "the great and terrible beast with its iron teeth and ten horns."** (*The Roman Republic began to rule as this fourth kingdom, after Macedonia was defeated in battle, and became a Roman province in 149 B.C.).*

Note: some historians will often separate the Macedonian Empire, from the Greek Empire, when they talk about the military conquests that were achieved, after the death of "Alexander the Great." However, it needs to be understood that Daniel does not separate this kingdom, in any way, and considers that the "Macedonian-Greek Empire" remained in power, until after Macedonia was defeated in battle, by the Roman Republic. This is when the Roman Republic, took its turn in power, and became the fourth kingdom. This fourth kingdom remained in power, for many centuries, which eventually evolved into the "Holy Roman Empire." And then in 1512, the name of this fourth kingdom was officially changed, and this is when it became the "Holy Roman Empire of the German Nation." Because this last title is often overlooked, in modern times, should explain why so many modern-day bible scholars have drawn the wrong conclusions, concerning the "Holy Roman Empire," and what role that this fourth kingdom would play, during the "last days."

Daniel 2:41-42

In 1805, another kingdom made its move, and this is when the fourth kingdom was defeated in battle. This is when the "First French Empire," under the rule of Napoleon Bonaparte, took its turn in power and became the fifth kingdom:

> **Daniel 2:41, "And whereas thou sawest the feet and toes, part of potters' clay, and part of iron, the kingdom shall be divided; but there shall be in it of the strength of the iron, forasmuch as thou sawest the iron mixed with miry clay."**

> **Daniel 2:42, "and as the toes of the feet were part of iron, and part of clay, so the kingdom shall be partly strong, and partly broken."**

Notice that this fifth kingdom is represented by **"the feet and toes, part of potters' clay, and part of iron."**

Note: because so many bible scholars, overlook the important role that Napoleon Bonaparte played, in fulfilling Daniel's "ten kings" prophecy, should explain why so many false theories are created, in modern times.

The most important clues that we need, to solve this prophecy, concerns the relationship that the "feet and toes" once had with the "legs of iron," and what role the kingdom of "clay" played, in fulfilling this prophecy: **"and as the toes of the feet were part of iron, and part of clay, so the kingdom shall be partly strong, and partly broken."** The **"legs of iron,"** represent the fourth kingdom, which was the "Holy Roman Empire of the German Nation." The "two feet made **"part of iron and part of clay"** represents the fifth kingdom, after the "First French Empire" defeated the "Holy Roman Empire of the German Nation," in battle. Because the "Holy Roman Empire of the German Nation" was represented by iron, provides proof that the "clay" would represent a completely different kingdom, not related in any way to the fourth kingdom.

For example: if we compare the fifth kingdom with the second and third kingdoms, represented by the silver and brass, and then ***combine*** these two metals together, we would have to conclude that the second and third kingdoms were somehow connected, and that these two empires ruled together: or the "Persian Empire" shared its power with the "Macedonian-Greek Empire." However, because the second and third empires are represented by silver and brass, which were never combined, together, in any way, proves that these two kingdoms ruled over their individual territories, separately.

With this understanding, we can now recognize that **"the feet and toes, part of potters' clay, and part of iron,"** represent two different and separate kingdoms, which would somehow share their power, and rule together. The "iron" represents the "Holy Roman Empire of the German Nation," while the "clay" represents the "First French Empire," under the rule of Napoleon Bonaparte.

The "ten toes" and "ten horns" represent the powerful monarchs, who ruled from within the "Holy Roman Empire of the German Nation," as the "League of the Rhine." The **"legs of iron,"** represents a very strong and powerful kingdom, while the **"potters' clay"** represents a very fragile kingdom: a kingdom, which would never be unified, or become very powerful. We learn this from the following scriptures:

> **"And as the toes of the feet were part of iron, and part of clay, so the kingdom shall be partly strong, and partly broken. And whereas thou sawest iron mixed with miry clay, they shall mingle themselves with the seed of men: but they shall not cleave one to another, even as iron is not mixed with clay"** (Daniel 2:42-43).

Because the feet, in this fifth kingdom, were made **"part of iron and part of clay,"** proves that the two feet once had a direct relationship with both kingdoms. Therefore, in accordance with this prophecy, the "First French Empire" (the fifth kingdom) would share its power with the ten powerful monarchs, who ruled from within the "Holy Roman Empire of the German Nation."

The fact that so many modern-day ministers and scholars, have completely overlooked this German connection, should explain why they fail to recognize that this prophecy was fulfilled, sometime during the nineteenth century. To this day, many ministers continue to teach their congregations that Daniel's "ten kings" prophecy will be fulfilled, sometime in the future, when "ten kings" in Europe will join forces to rule the world. However, the fact that very few nations in Europe are ruled by Kings and Queens, in modern times, proves that the reign of the powerful monarchs ended, a long time ago. Therefore, this provides proof that this prophecy was fulfilled, during the time when many nations in Europe were governed, by the powerful monarchs. The whole idea that Daniel's "ten kings" prophecy will be fulfilled, sometime in the future, is a complete fallacy.

As soon as Napoleon defeated the "Holy Roman Empire of the German Nation," in battle, is when the reign of the fourth kingdom came to an end. This fourth kingdom was officially removed from power, after the "treaty of Pressburg" was signed, December 26, 1805. Eight months later, on August 6, 1806, Francis II (the last "Holy Roman Emperor" and the "Emperor of Austria") decided to completely dissolve the "Holy Roman Empire of the German Nation." It was this military defeat of the fourth kingdom, which fulfilled the first part of the prophecy in the "Book of Revelation" (Revelation 13:3), which proclaims that **"one of his heads"** was **"wounded to death."**

"And I saw one of his heads as it were wounded to death; and his deadly wound was healed: and all the world wondered after the beast" (Revelation 13:3).

This prophecy is talking about the crest of the "Holy Roman Empire," which was a "Two Headed Black Eagle," that represented the "Holy Roman Empire" for many centuries. The first part of this prophecy: **"And I saw one of his heads as it were wounded to death"** was fulfilled, after Napoleon defeated the "Holy Roman Empire of the German Nation," in battle. However, it should also be remembered that this prophecy also predicted: **"and his deadly wound was healed,"** which provides proof that this fourth kingdom was scheduled to rise to power again, sometime after 1806.

After Napoleon defeated this fourth kingdom, he then began to reorganize the powerful monarchs, who ruled from within the "League of the Rhine." This league of kings was originally created to protect the cities and villages along the Rhine River, and keep the power of the "Holy Roman Empire," under control. Napoleon made several political changes, to this monarch line, and renamed it the "Confederation of the Rhine." This is when the kingdom of "clay," shared its power with the powerful monarchs, who once ruled from within the kingdom of "iron." This explains why the fifth kingdom was made **"part of iron and part of clay."** Therefore, as soon as Napoleon began to share his power with the "Confederation of the Rhine," in 1806, is when Daniel's "ten kings" prophecy *began* to be fulfilled.

The "Confederation of the Rhine"

THE "LEAGUE OF the Rhine" was originally created in 1658, which consisted of several powerful Monarchs, and princes. In 1806, Napoleon reorganized this powerful monarch organization, and renamed it the "Confederation of the Rhine." It was comprised of nine kings and the college of 28 princes. The president of this newly formed confederation (the tenth king) was Karl Theodor Von Dalberg, who was the Arch Chancellor in the "Holy Roman Empire," and the Arch Bishop of Mainz. This appointment cemented the religious connection, between the **"the legs of iron,"** and the **"two feet and ten toes."** This is because Karl Theodor Von Dalberg was not only the Arch Bishop of Mainz, but he was also one of the original *seven electors,* who voted from within the "Holy Roman Empire." The *seven electors* were once responsible for choosing who the next "King of the Romans" should be. This chosen individual would then become the new "Holy Roman Emperor," as soon as he is officially crowned, by the Pope. Even though this practice ended, after Charles V was crowned in 1530, the "Book of Revelation" still refers to these seven electors as the seven heads with seven crowns; the ten kings as the ten horns; the "Holy Roman Empire" as the terrible beast; the "Holy Roman Catholic Church" as the great red dragon; and the Pope as the dragon who speaks blasphemies (study Revelation 12:3; 13:1; 13:6-8 for clarity).

The "First French Empire," under Napoleon Bonaparte, was a very strong military power that lasted from 1805 until June 18, 1815, when he was defeated at Waterloo. Many of these kings continued to rule, even though the "Confederation of the Rhine" was officially dissolved in 1813, after the Battle of Leipzig (October 16-19, 1813). These kings remained in power, until after the European Revolutions ended, in 1848. Therefore, the timetable for when these powerful kings ruled, began in 1806 and ended in 1848. When the bible uses the phrase **"iron mixed with miry clay,"** and proclaims that **"they shall not cleave one to another, even as iron is not mixed with clay,"** this accurately describes the stormy relationship that existed between France, and the powerful monarchs, who ruled from within the "Confederation of the Rhine." Napoleon shared his power with these powerful monarchs, because he wanted to create a long lasting and unified government, throughout Europe. In fact, after the rule of Napoleon Bonaparte ended, France tried many more times, but failed to unite the Europeans under one strong and powerful government. Because this unification process was never achieved, confirms that the prophecies: **"but they shall not cleave one to another, even as iron is not mixed with clay"** and **"the kingdom shall be partly strong, and partly broken"** were fulfilled, during that time.

There is one more important clue, to consider, when deciding exactly when Daniel's "ten kings" prophecy was fulfilled. It needs to be understood that every time one kingdom, was removed from power, the next kingdom *immediately* took its turn in power. It was no different after the "First French Empire" defeated the fourth kingdom, in battle, and *immediately* took its turn in power as the fifth kingdom (the kingdom of clay). In fact, the "Confederation of the Rhine" was created in July 1806, and in August 1806, the "Holy Roman Empire of the German

Nation" was dissolved. To this day, many bible scholars fail to recognize the important clues, which reveal exactly when and how this prophecy was fulfilled. As a result, many Christians continue to be taught that this prophecy will be fulfilled, sometime in the future. However, this theory completely ignores the fact that every kingdom *immediately* took its turn in power, as soon as the previous empire was defeated, in battle:

Therefore, as soon as the first empire was defeated, in battle, the second empire **immediately** took control. As soon as the second empire was defeated, in battle, the third empire **immediately** took control, and so forth and so on.

It was no different when the "First French Empire" *immediately* took its turn in power, and became the fifth kingdom, as soon as it defeated the fourth kingdom (the "Holy Roman Empire of the German Nation") in battle, in December 1805.

Understand; the fact that every kingdom **immediately** took control, soon after the previous kingdom was removed from power, provides proof that every prophecy in Nebuchadnezzar's dream was fulfilled, after the rule of these powerful kings ended, in 1848. Therefore, Nebuchadnezzar's dream did not offer any more predictions for the future. His dream did not offer any prophecy for the "League of Nations," which came to power after World War I, with 63 members: or for the United Nations, with its 193 members: or for the "European Economic Community" (EEC) with its 32 members. The fact that none of these organizations were even mentioned in Nebuchadnezzar's dream, provides proof that every prophecy was fulfilled, after the European Revolutions ended in 1848. Therefore, the whole concept that ten kings in Europe, would someday combine their power together, and rule the world, is just one more false interpretation of Daniel's prophecies.

And this is where the next prophecy comes into play:

Daniel 2:44

"And in the days of these kings shall the God of heaven set up a kingdom, which shall never be destroyed: and the kingdom shall not be left to other people, but it shall break in pieces and consume all these kingdoms, and it shall stand forever" (Daniel 2:44).

It is interesting to note, that even though many theories have been created, concerning the fourth kingdom, very few people have even attempted to explain when or how this prophecy (Daniel 2:44) was fulfilled. We learn from this prophecy that the "Kingdom of God" was predicted to be established, on earth, sometime during the reign of the "ten kings." Because the "ten kings" ruled between the years of 1806 and 1848, proves that the "Kingdom of God" had to be established, somewhere on earth, during that time. It needs to be understood that even though the fifth kingdom was defeated in battle, in 1815, the French Empire remained in power until after the French Revolution of 1830 ended, which removed King Charles X from power. Therefore, this provides proof that the sixth kingdom would have taken its turn in power, sometime in 1830, slightly before the French Revolution ended in July.

The fact that most modern-day ministers fail to recognize the official "Kingdom of God," on earth, today, should concern every Christian around the world. How would it be possible for any **true minister** of God, not recognize God's True Church, whether he can explain the bible prophecies, or not? Is it possible that the modern-day ministers, today, are the blind ministers that Christians were previously warned about? Are they the blind leading the blind?

"And he spake a parable unto them, Can the blind lead the blind? Shall they not both fall into the ditch?" (Luke 6:39).

The fact that Daniel's "ten kings" prophecy was fulfilled, sometime between the years of 1806 and 1848, raises several serious questions, concerning the Christian denominations that exist, in modern times. For example: we learn from the historical record that the Catholic Church was established sometime during the first century A.D., while most Protestant churches were established, during the sixteenth and seventeenth centuries. Therefore, the historical records prove, that these churches were established several centuries before Daniel's "ten kings" was fulfilled. When we consider that most ministers cannot even recognize the official "Kingdom of God" (God's True Church) on earth, today, provides more proof that something is wrong. Is it possible that the answer, to this question, is fully explained in the following scripture?

"Surely the Lord God will do nothing, but he revealeth his secret unto his servants the prophets" (Amos 3:7).

Therefore, we should require that every modern-day minister explain, why they were not notified by God, or by the Holy Spirit, when the official "Kingdom of God" was established, on earth. Maybe they should also explain, why they cannot recognize the official "Kingdom of God" on earth, today? The fact that only one denomination, fulfilled Daniel's "Kingdom of God" prophecy (Daniel 2:44), proves that every other denomination would be counterfeit. The counterfeit churches are filled with many blind ministers, who are leading their congregations down the wrong path, and right into a ditch: just like Jesus explained in his parable (Luke 6:39).

The Sixth Kingdom

It needs to be understood, that considerable confusion exists, today, concerning exactly when and how the "Kingdom of God" would be established, on earth. As a result, many ministers teach their congregations that every Christian will know when the "Kingdom of God" is established, on earth, because this will happen *after* Jesus returns. However, this theory contradicts what the bible teaches. We learn from Daniel that the "Kingdom of God" was scheduled to be established, on earth, sometime during the reign of the "ten kings." Because Daniel's "ten kings" prophecy was fulfilled, between the years of 1806 and 1848, provides proof that the "Kingdom of God" prophecy (Daniel 2:44) was fulfilled, during that time. The fact that the fifth kingdom was removed from power, in July 1830, provides even more proof that the sixth kingdom took its turn in power, slightly before that time. Because so many ministers cannot recognize the official "Kingdom of God" on earth, today, provides proof that most ministers know nothing about the "latter-day" prophecies, or can even explain when or how Daniel's prophecies were fulfilled. In the following scripture we learn that Jesus will return like **"a thief in the night:"**

> **"For yourselves know perfectly that the day of the Lord so cometh as a thief in the night"** (1 Thessalonians 5:2).

If the bible teaches that Jesus will return, like **"a thief in the night,"** then what does this reveal about God's True Church? Do you think that the official "Kingdom of God" would be established, on earth, so the entire world could easily destroy it? This danger made it imperative that God's True Church be established, on earth, in such a manner, that this church would not immediately be recognized as the official "Kingdom of God." This would then protect the faithful followers and give them time to build up membership in the church. Understand; the "Kingdom of God," on earth, is simply another name for God's True Church, which is also the true Church of Jesus Christ. This is explained, in the following scriptures, when we study about the **"stone,"** and the relationship that this **"stone"** has with God's True Church.

> **"Forasmuch as thou sawest that the STONE was cut out of the mountain without hands, and that it brake in pieces the iron, the brass, the clay, the silver, and the gold; the great God hath made known to the king what shall come to pass hereafter: and the dream is certain, and the interpretation thereof sure"** (Daniel 2:45).

> **"Thou sawest till that a STONE was cut out without hands, which smote the image upon his feet that were of iron and clay, and brake them to pieces. Then was the iron, the clay, the brass, the silver, and the gold, broken to pieces together, and became like the chaff of the summer threshing floors; and the wind carried them away, that no place was found for them: and the STONE that smote the image became a great mountain, and filled the whole earth"** (Daniel 2:34-35).

The **"stone"** which **"was cut without hands,"** is referring to Jesus Christ as the "stone of Israel," which also includes the true gospel that Jesus taught: **"Forasmuch as thou sawest that the STONE was cut**

out of the mountain without hands." The second half of this prophecy: **"and that it brake in pieces the iron, the brass, the clay, the silver, and the gold,"** is letting us know that the other five kingdoms will be out of power, when God's True Church takes its place as the sixth kingdom, on earth.

We are then told: **"and the STONE that smote the image became a great mountain, and filled the whole earth."** In other words, God's True Church and the "True Gospel of Jesus Christ, will eventually spread around the world, while the other five kingdoms will only be remembered in the history books: **"and the wind carried them away, that no place was found for them."**

Note: because the fifth kingdom, was removed from power during the French Revolution in July 1830, provides proof that the "Kingdom of God" (sixth kingdom) was established, on earth, slightly before July of that year. This confirms that the other powerful kingdoms were not in power, by the time the sixth kingdom took its turn in power, in 1830, which fulfilled the prophecy: **"and the wind carried them away, that no place was found for them."**

We learn more about the **"stone"** in the following scriptures:

> **"Be it known unto you all, and to all the people of Israel, that by the name Jesus Christ of Nazareth, whom ye crucified, whom God raised from the dead, even by him doth this man stand here before you whole. This is the STONE which was set at nought of you builders, which is become the HEAD OF THE CORNER. Neither is there salvation in any other: for there is none other name under heaven given among men, whereby we must be saved"** (Acts 4:10-12).
>
> **"And he beheld them, and said, What is this then that is**

written, The STONE which the builders rejected, the same is become the HEAD OF THE CORNER? Whosoever shall fall upon that STONE shall be broken; but on whomsoever it shall fall, it will grind him to powder" (Luke 20: 17-18).

"And have ye not read this scripture; The STONE which the builders rejected is become THE HEAD OF THE CORNER:" (Mark 12:10).

The **"chief corner stone,"** and **"the head of the corner"** is also mentioned, in the following scriptures:

"And are built upon the foundation of the apostles and prophets, JESUS CHRIST HIMSELF BEING THE CHIEF CORNER STONE; In whom all the building fitly framed together groweth unto an holy temple in the Lord: In whom ye also are builded together for an habitation of God through the Spirit" (Ephesians 2:20-22).

In other words, the **"stone"** is Jesus Christ, who is also the **"chief corner stone"** of the Church of Jesus Christ, which is also **"built upon the foundation of the apostles and prophets."**

Daniel 2:34-35

We learn from Daniel's "Kingdom of God" prophecy (Daniel 2:44), that sometime during the reign of the "ten kings," the sixth kingdom was established on earth. In the following prophecy, we learn that this sixth kingdom is the **"stone"** that **"was cut out without hands"** (God's True Church), which will eventually spread around the world:

> **"Thou sawest till that a STONE WAS CUT OUT WITHOUT HANDS, which smote the image upon his feet that were of iron and clay, and brake them to pieces and the stone that smote the image became a great mountain, AND FILLED THE WHOLE EARTH"** (Daniel 2:34).

We then learn that the other kingdoms will become as important as the chaff on the threshing floors: **"like the chaff of the summer threshing floors:"**

> **"Then was the iron, the clay, the brass, the silver, and the gold, broken to pieces together, AND BECAME LIKE THE CHAFF OF THE SUMMER THRESHING FLOORS; and the wind carried them away, that no place was found for

them: and the STONE that smote the image became a great mountain, and filled the whole earth" (Daniel 2:35).

This prophecy is explaining that even though the other five kingdoms were once very powerful kingdoms, they will become as important as the **"chaff,"** which is separated from the wheat and cast away. These five kingdoms will be forgotten, and will only be remembered, in the history books: **"and the wind carried them away, that no place was found for them."**

Sadly, most Christians are completely unaware that the official "Kingdom of God" was established, on earth, between the years of 1806 and 1848. The fact that most Christians have not been taught the difference between the "Kingdom of God **on earth,**" and the "Kingdom of God **in heaven,**" should also explain why so many Christians will continue to remain skeptical. Understand; after Jesus returns, the "Kingdom of God" ***on earth*** (God's True Church), will then receive the full authority of the "Kingdom of God" ***in heaven.*** This is when the True Church of Jesus Christ will receive the full authority from God, to rule the world, with Jesus Christ. This transfer of authority will happen during the **"marriage of the Lamb."** Therefore, if God's True Church does not exist on earth, before Jesus returns, then how would it be possible for the **"marriage of the Lamb"** to be performed?

The Marriage of the Lamb

"Let us be glad and rejoice, and give honour to him: for the marriage of the Lamb is come, and his wife hath made herself ready. And to her was granted that she should be arrayed in fine linen, clean and white: for the fine linen is the righteousness of saints. And he saith unto me, Write, Blessed are they which are called unto the marriage supper of the Lamb. And he saith unto me, These are the true sayings of God" (Revelation 19:7-9).

THE BRIDE IN this prophecy, is talking about the official "Kingdom of God" **on earth** (God's True Church), which was established, during the reign of the "ten kings" (Daniel 2:44). As soon as this church was established, it began to fulfill the "restoration" prophecies, which also included restoring the "True Gospel of Jesus Christ," on earth. Understand; only one church fulfilled Daniel's prophecies, and received the official authority from God, to carry out this assignment. The fact that the modern-day churches disagree, on a wide range of religious issues, proves that the Christian community is divided, concerning how the scriptures should be interpreted and taught. How would it be possible for any disagreements to occur, if every denomination received the authority from God, to teach the truth? The fact that the Holy

Spirit will only teach the truth, proves that ONLY ONE CORRECT INTERPRETATION OF THE BIBLE SCRIPTURES exists, which also proves that ONLY ONE CHURCH on earth, today, is teaching the Real Gospel Truth with the power of the Holy Ghost.

In the following scriptures, we learn that God's authority cannot be divided up, and then shared among the other churches (or denominations), without dividing the "Kingdom of God," against itself.

> **"And Jesus knew their thoughts, and said unto them, Every kingdom divided against itself is brought to desolation; and every city or house divided against itself shall not stand"** (Matthew 12:25).

> **"And if a kingdom be divided against itself, that kingdom cannot stand"** (Mark 3:24).

> **"But he, knowing their thoughts, said unto them, Every kingdom divided against itself is brought to desolation; and a house divided against a house falleth"** (Luke 11:17).

Understand; dividing the authority of God, or the Holy Priesthood, is the same thing as dividing the "Kingdom of God," against itself. Therefore, this should also explain why it would not be possible for more than one church, on earth, to receive the official authority from God, to teach the gospel. Only ONE church would receive this authority. Only ONE church is teaching the correct interpretation, of the bible scriptures, with the power of the Holy Ghost.

During the ministry of Jesus, the temple in Jerusalem received the full authority of the Holy Priesthood, which officially established the "Kingdom of God" on earth, during that time. The fact that Jesus established his church, on earth, during his ministry, should explain why

"John the Baptist" began his ministry 3½ years before Jesus arrived, in Jerusalem. John was simply building up membership, in the Church of Jesus Christ, before Jesus arrived. Because the ministry of "John the Baptist" was so successful, explains why a great multitude of people were gathered, anxiously waiting for the arrival of their Messiah:

> **"And a VERY GREAT MULTITUDE spread their garments in the way; others cut down branches from the trees, and strawed them in the way. And the multitudes that went before, and that followed, cried, saying, Hosanna to the Son of David: Blessed is he that cometh in the name of the Lord; Hosanna in the highest"** (Matthew 21:8-9).

Because it was important for Jesus to build up membership, in his church, before he began his ministry, provides proof that he would do the same thing, during the "last days," *before* he returns. His true church would then be established, on earth, sometime during the "last days," so Christians will have enough time to get prepared, for his return. During this process, the Church of Jesus Christ will then receive the full authority of the Holy Priesthood, which will authorize this church to "restore" everything back to the way that it needs to be, before Jesus returns. This will also include "restoring" the true gospel of Jesus Christ on earth.

Even though many ministers will often proclaim that they teach the true gospel, they do not have the "restored" gospel of Jesus Christ, in their possession. For example: we learn from the "Old Testament" scriptures, that Jesus was predicted to be born, on earth, and would also be crucified (Isaiah 53). In the "New Testament" we learn about the birth of Jesus; his ministry; and his crucifixion. In the "restored" gospel, which most ministers do not have, we learn what happened after Jesus resurrected; the places that he visited; and the people that he taught. The fact that most modern-day ministers know nothing about these scriptures, or what happened after Jesus resurrected, provides proof that they do not have the "restored" gospel, in their possession.

To prove, which church is the official "Kingdom of God" on earth, today, is a very simple process. It needs to be understood that this church would have to fulfill the following prophecies:

1. This church would have to be established, on earth, sometime during the reign of the "ten kings," and slightly before the European Revolutions ended in 1848.
2. This church would also have to be established, before Daniel's "sanctuary be cleansed" prophecy was fulfilled, **on earth.**
3. This church would also have to teach the "restored" gospel of Jesus Christ.
4. This church would also have to fulfill: **"And it shall come to pass in the last days, that the mountain of the Lord's house shall be established in the top of the mountains, and shall be exalted above the hills; and all nations shall flow unto it"** (Isaiah 2;2 and Micah 4:1).

As you can see, these four prophecies would make it rather difficult for any denomination to fake, and especially when we have the historical record to study. The historical record can easily prove which denomination is telling the truth.

Because we now understand that the official "Kingdom of God" was established on earth, sometime between the years of 1806 and 1848, we can now use Daniel's timetable to determine which church (or denomination) fulfilled Daniel's prophecies. Therefore, any Christian church established before 1806, or any time after 1848, would not qualify as the official "Kingdom of God" on earth, today. See how simple?

To see if your church can pass this test, or not, is a very simple process. The first step is to find out what year your church (or denomination) was officially established, and then compare this date with Daniel's timetable, to see if this date would fit between the years of 1806 and 1848. Keep in mind that all separations and divisions, would also be a deciding factor, in determining what year your church was officially established. The fact that most Protestant denominations were established, during the sixteenth and seventeenth centuries, proves that most Protestant denominations would fail this test. However, because we have so many different Protestant denominations, today, makes it feasible that a few could possibly match Daniel's timetable. Understand; even though this would be possible, this denomination would still have to prove that it fulfilled the other three prophecies, which we previously discussed.

Because the Catholic Church was established sometime during the first century A.D., which was many centuries before Daniel's "ten kings" prophecy was fulfilled, proves that this church fails this test.

Because the Jehovah Witness Church was officially established by Charles Taze Russell, in 1872, several years after Daniel's "ten kings" prophecy was fulfilled, also proves that this denomination fails this test.

Because the Seventh-Day Adventist Church was officially established on May 21, 1863, several years after Daniel's "ten kings" prophecy was fulfilled, also proves that this denomination fails this test.

Because "The Church of Jesus Christ of Latter-day Saints" was officially established on April 6, 1830, proves that this church was established between the years of 1806 and 1848. Therefore, because this church matches Daniel's timetable, we must now do the necessary research, to find out if this church fulfilled the other bible prophecies:

1. Is there any proof, that this church fulfilled Daniel's "sanctuary be cleansed" prophecy, **on earth?**
2. Does this church have the "Restored Gospel of Jesus Christ" in its possession?
3. Does this church fulfill the prophecy: **"And it shall come to pass in the last days, that the mountain of the Lord's house shall be established in the top of the mountains, and shall be exalted above the hills; and all nations shall flow unto it"** (Isaiah 2;2 and Micah 4:1)?

When discussing "The Church of Jesus Christ of Latter-day Saints," we must not forget to also discuss Prophet Joseph Smith, so that we can determine what role (if any) that he would have played in fulfilling the "latter-day" prophecies.

In the following scriptures we learn that God will never change:

"FOR I AM THE LORD, I CHANGE NOT; therefore ye sons of Jacob are not consumed" (Malachi 3:6).

"Jesus Christ the same yesterday, and today, and forever" (Hebrews 13:8).

Therefore, because God will never change, provides proof that God will use the same methods, during the "last days," that he always used in the past. The fact that God sent many prophets, in the past, like: Abraham, Daniel, Ezra, Isaac, Jacob, Joseph, Elijah, Elisha, Isaiah, Jeremiah, Ezekiel, Amos, Jonah, Micah, Malachi, and many more, proves that he would do the same thing again, during the "last days." In fact, we learn from the bible scriptures that God always sent a prophet, before something important happens on earth. What event could possibly be more important than the return of Jesus Christ? Would this event be important enough, for God to intervene, and send another prophet to prepare the people on earth, for the return of Jesus? To fully understand the role that the prophets played, during biblical times, it needs to be understood that Moses was not only sent to lead the Israelites out of Egypt (Exodus 3), but that he was also sent to teach the Israelites about God's laws, and commandments. It was during the exodus when Moses bestowed the priesthood authority upon Aaron, and his sons (Exodus 40:15), and when he gave the Israelites the "Ten Commandments" (Deuteronomy 4:13). None of these things would have been possible without a prophet.

In the following scriptures, we learn that God often spoke to his people, through his chosen prophets:

> "I have also SPOKEN BY THE PROPHETS, and I have multiplied visions, and used similitudes, by the MINISTRY OF THE PROPHETS" (Hosea 12:10).

> "God, who at sundry times and in divers manners SPAKE in time past unto the fathers BY THE PROPHETS" (Hebrews 1:1).

> "And the LORD God of their fathers sent to them by HIS MESSENGER, rising up betimes, and sending; because he had compassion on his people, and on his dwelling place" (2 Chronicles 36:15).

In fact, we learn from Amos that God will do nothing, unless he notifies his prophets first:

> "Surely the Lord god WILL DO NOTHING, but he revealeth his secret unto his servants the prophets" (Amos 3:7).

Therefore, is it possible that Prophet Joseph Smith was a "latter-day" prophet, who received the priesthood authority to establish God's True Church on earth, during the "last days?"

When we study Daniel's timetable, we discover that this prophet had to be born sometime before the "ten kings" were placed in power, in 1806, or sometime during their reign. In either case, this prophet would also have to remain on earth, until the "sanctuary be cleansed" prophecy is fulfilled. The fact that Joseph Smith was born December 23, 1805, proves that he was born slightly before the "ten kings" were placed in power, in 1806. Therefore, the next question we need to investigate, concerns the role (if any) that Joseph Smith would have played, in fulfilling Daniel's "sanctuary be cleansed" prophecy, **on earth**.

Daniel's "Sanctuary be Cleansed" Prophecy

What role did "The Church of Jesus Christ of Latter-day Saints" play, in fulfilling Daniel's "sanctuary be cleansed" prophecy, on earth? We learn from Daniel exactly when the "cleansing" of the "sanctuary" was scheduled to be fulfilled. When we compare the historical record, with this prophecy, we should be able to find some evidence that this prophecy was fulfilled, on earth, right on schedule. The fact that so many ministers failed to recognize the fulfillment of Daniel's "ten kings" prophecy, when it was fulfilled, should explain why they also missed the fulfillment of Daniel's "sanctuary be cleansed" prophecy. This is where the false interpretations, concerning Daniel's "sanctuary be cleansed" prophecy, comes into play.

In the early 1800's, there was a Baptist minister by the name of William Miller, who became very interested in one prophecy that he discovered, in the "Book of Daniel." This prophecy reads as follows:

> "Then I heard one saint speaking, and another saint said unto that certain saint which spake, How long shall be the vision concerning the daily sacrifice, and the transgression of desolation, to give both the sanctuary and the host to

be trodden under foot? And he said unto me, Unto two thousand and three hundred days; then shall the sanctuary be cleansed"** (Daniel 8:13-14).

After Mr. Miller studied this prophecy, he then concluded that this prophecy was providing an accurate timetable, for exactly when Jesus would return to earth, to begin his millennial rule. He arrived at this conclusion after he studied the following words: **"then shall the sanctuary be cleansed."** Mr. Miller theorized that if the earth was the "sanctuary," then this would mean that the entire world would be "cleansed," in 2300 days (years), from some unspecified date. As a result, he also theorized that this "cleansing" process could only be fulfilled, *after* Jesus returns. He possibly arrived, at this conclusion, after studying the following scripture:

"But the day of the Lord will come as a thief in the night; in the which the heavens shall pass away with a great noise, and the elements shall melt with fervent heat, the earth also and the works that are therein shall be burned up" (2 Peter 3:10).

As you can see, it would not be very difficult to assume that the entire world would be "cleansed," *after* Jesus returns. This "cleansing" process would begin as soon as **"the heavens shall pass away,"** and **"the elements shall melt with fervent heat, the earth also."** The earth would be completely "cleansed," because nothing would exist, anywhere on earth, after this prophecy is fulfilled. Therefore, after Mr. Miller made some mathematical calculations, he then concluded that this event was scheduled to happen, sometime in 1843. When this event did not happen in 1843, as he expected, he then rechecked his mathematics for accuracy, and discovered that he made a slight error in his calculations.

Note: he possibly overlooked the missing zero-year.

After correcting his error, he then announced that this event would be fulfilled, no later than October 22, 1844. The fact that we can now look back in history, and plainly see that Jesus did not return, during that time, proves that something was wrong with Mr. Miller's theory. Today, this theory would be recognized, by most Christians, as being another "Rapture" theory. In other words, Mr. Miller was simply predicting that the "Rapture" would happen, sometime in 1844.

In either case, Mr. Miller made several serious errors, and false assumptions, when he created his theory. The first error concerned the return of Jesus. He should have known that any theory, which predicted exactly when Jesus would return to earth, would have to be false, simply because of the following scripture:

"But of that day and that hour knoweth no man, no, not the angels which are in heaven, neither the Son, but the Father" (Mark 13:32).

The second error that he made, concerns the "cleansing" of the "sanctuary," and how this prophecy would be fulfilled. Therefore, he failed to understand that Daniel was talking about an event, which would only be fulfilled, sometime after the "Kingdom of God" (God's True Church) is established, on earth. This is when a spiritual "cleansing" would be needed, to sanctify and spiritually "cleanse" the official "Kingdom of God," on earth. The fact that he failed to understand how this spiritual "cleansing" would be accomplished, should explain why he also assumed that this prophecy could only be fulfilled, after Jesus returns.

As you can imagine, as soon as Mr. Miller published his theory, in the media, the country went wild with excitement. Many Christians were convinced that Jesus was on his way. However, when Jesus did not return before October 22, 1844, as expected, this date became known as the "Great Disappointment." The fact that so many Christians believed Mr. Miller's theory, also caused many Christians to lose their faith, because they were convinced that God let them down. Sadly, and to this day, Christians have not been taught the truth, concerning this prophecy, and how this prophecy was fulfilled, *on earth,* right on schedule.

Daniel's "sanctuary be cleansed" prophecy reads as follows:

> **"Then I heard one saint speaking, and another saint said unto that certain saint which spake, How long shall be the vision concerning the daily sacrifice, and the transgression of desolation, to give both the sanctuary and the host to be trodden under foot? and he said unto me, unto two thousand and three hundred days; then shall the sanctuary be cleansed"** (Daniel 8:13-14).

Here are the five clues, that we were given, to solve this prophecy:

1. **"the vision concerning the daily sacrifice,"**
2. **"the transgression of desolation,"**
3. **"both the sanctuary and the host to be trodden under foot?"**
4. **"two thousand and three hundred days"** (meaning: 2300 years);
5. **"then shall the sanctuary be cleansed."**

The first clue: **"the vision concerning the daily sacrifice"** is referring to the crucifixion of Jesus, which permanently abolished the daily animal blood sacrifices, for the remission of sins. Therefore, it is the blood sacrifice that Jesus made, which **"cleanseth us from all sin,"** today:

> **"But if we walk in the light, as he is in the light, we have fellowship one with another, and THE BLOOD OF JESUS**

CHRIST HIS SON CLEANSETH US FROM ALL SIN" (1 John 1:7).

The second clue: concerning the **"transgression of desolation,"** is talking about the **"transgression"** of the people, when they rejected the true gospel of Jesus Christ, which caused the **"desolation"** (the apostasy) to spread around the world, just like Amos predicted (Amos 8). Their punishment began as soon as the temple, in Jerusalem, was destroyed.

The third clue: **"both the sanctuary and the host to be trodden under foot,"** is talking about the apostasy (the "spiritual darkness"), which allows God's **"sanctuary"** (the temple) and the **"host"** (Jesus Christ) to be **"trodden under foot."** We then learn from the fourth and fifth clues, that this disrespect would continue for 2300 years, until the prophecy: **"then shall the sanctuary be cleansed"** is fulfilled.

Earlier, when we discussed the prophecies of Daniel, in chapter nine (Daniel 9:26 and 9:27), and the prophecy of Amos (Amos 8), we discovered that the entire world was covered in "spiritual darkness," shortly after the temple in Jerusalem was destroyed, in 70 A.D. It should also be remembered that Amos also predicted that this is when, the true gospel that Jesus taught (the **"words of the Lord"**), was lost.

In the following scripture, we learn that this worldwide apostasy (a "falling way") was predicted to happen, before Jesus returns:

> **"Let no man deceive you by any means: FOR THAT DAY SHALL NOT COME, except there come a falling away first, and that man of sin be revealed, the son of perdition"** (2 Thessalonians 2:3).

The phrase **"falling away,"** simply means to "fall away" from the laws, and commandments of God. In fact, we learn from this scripture that Jesus will not return (**"for that day shall not come"**), until after this "falling away" prophecy, is fulfilled. Because we now understand that the apostasy began to spread around the world, shortly after 70 A.D., provides proof that this **"falling away"** prophecy was fulfilled, many years ago. Therefore, this proves that Jesus can now return to earth, at any time.

When studying the fourth and fifth clues, concerning the **"two thousand and three hundred days; then shall the sanctuary be cleansed"** we learn that after a total of 2300 days (years) have passed (from some unspecified date), the "sanctuary" will then be "cleansed."

Here is this prophecy again:

> **"Then I heard one saint speaking, and another saint said unto that certain saint which spake, How long shall be the vision concerning the daily sacrifice, and the transgression of desolation, to give both the sanctuary and the host to be trodden under foot? and he said unto me, UNTO TWO THOUSAND AND THREE HUNDRED DAYS; THEN SHALL THE SANCTUARY BE CLEANSED"** (Daniel 8:13-14).

Therefore, one saint is simply asking the other saint a question: **"How long shall be the vision concerning the daily sacrifice, and the transgression of desolation, to give both the sanctuary and the host to be trodden under foot?** In other words: "how long will this "spiritual darkness" (the apostasy) remain, on earth, which allows **"the sanctuary and the host to be trodden under foot?"** The other saint then replies: **"unto two thousand and three hundred days; then shall the sanctuary be cleansed."** From this answer, we learn that in 2300 days (years), from some unspecified date, the "cleansing" of the "sanctuary" will be fulfilled, and this is when **"the sanctuary and the host to be trodden under foot"** will come to an end. In other words, the fulfillment of Daniel's "sanctuary be cleansed" prophecy, in 2300 days, will end the world-wide apostasy (the "spiritual darkness"), which began to spread around the world, shortly after 70 A.D.

Here is what Daniel was predicting:

> **First: the "Kingdom of God" would be established on earth, sometime during the reign of the fifth kingdom, after the "ten kings" are placed in power.**
>
> **Second: in 2300 days (years), from some unspecified date, God's "sanctuary" will then be "cleansed," which will end "the overspreading of abominations" and end: "the sanctuary and the host to be trodden under foot." In other words, this is when the "spiritual darkness" (the apostasy) will begin to be removed, from earth.**

As you can see, this is quite different from what Mr. Miller predicted, when he announced that Jesus was returning to earth, to begin his millennial rule. The fact that Mr. Miller, and many others, missed the fulfillment of Daniel's "ten kings" prophecy, caused them to also miss the fulfillment of Daniel's "sanctuary be cleansed" prophecy, when it was fulfilled **on earth,** right on schedule. How was it possible that so many ministers missed the fulfillment of this important prophecy, when they knew exactly what year that this prophecy, would be fulfilled? The simple fact that they had their eyes focused on the heavens, waiting and watching for the return of Jesus, should explain why they failed to recognize the event, which fulfilled this prophecy.

The "Cleansing" and the "Sanctuary"

Before it would be possible to begin deciphering Daniel's "sanctuary be cleansed" prophecy, we must first learn what the word "cleansed" means, when used in the religious context as: **"sanctuary be cleansed?"**

When spiritual "cleansings" were performed, during "Old Testament" times, it required that animals be sacrificed, so their blood could be sprinkled on the people and other objects. Therefore, the only way that a spiritual "cleansing" could be achieved, was through a physical blood sacrifice, made on earth. In the following scripture, we learn that blood plays a very important role, in the atonement for the soul:

> **"For the life of the flesh is in the blood: and I have given it to you upon the altar to make an atonement for your souls: for it is the blood that maketh an atonement for the soul,"** (Leviticus 17:11).

In the next scripture, we learn that blood sacrifices were often made to spiritually "cleanse" the people, from their sins:

> **"For on that day shall the priest make an atonement for**

you, to cleanse you, THAT YE MAY BE CLEAN FROM ALL YOUR SINS before the LORD" (Leviticus 16:30).

And to also "cleanse" the altar:

> "And he said unto me, Son of man, thus saith the Lord God; These are the ORDINANCES OF THE ALTAR in the day when they shall make it, to offer burnt offerings thereon, and to sprinkle blood thereon" (Ezekiel 43:18).

And was also performed, to "cleanse" the "sanctuary," itself:

> "Thus saith the Lord God; In the first month, in the first day of the month, thou shalt take a young bullock without blemish, and CLEANSE THE SANCTUARY" (Ezekiel 45:18).

In fact, we learn from the bible scriptures that the only way a spiritual "cleansing" could be achieved, is through a physical blood sacrifice (or atonement) made on earth. In the following scriptures, we learn that blood atonements were often made, for several different reasons:

> "And he shall make an atonement for the holy sanctuary, and he shall make an atonement for the tabernacle of the congregation, and for the altar, and he shall make an atonement for the priests, and for all the people of the congregation" (Leviticus 16:33).

Notice that these blood atonements were made for:

1. "the tabernacle of the congregation"
2. "the altar"
3. "the priests"
4. "and for all the people of the congregation"

In the "New Testament" we learn that Moses sprinkled his book with a mixture of **"BLOOD from calves, goats, water, and scarlet wool."**

> **"For when Moses had spoken every precept to all the people according to the law, he took the BLOOD of calves and of goats, with water, and scarlet wool, and hyssop, and sprinkled both the book, and all the people. Saying, This is the BLOOD OF THE TESTAMENT which God hath enjoined unto you. Moreover he sprinkled with BLOOD both the tabernacle, and all the vessels of the ministry. And ALMOST ALL THINGS ARE BY THE LAW PURGED WITH BLOOD; and without shedding of BLOOD is no remission"** (Hebrews 9:19-22).

Take special notice, that this scripture says: **"And almost all things are by the law purged with blood; and without shedding of blood is no remission"** (Hebrews 9:22). This verse is explaining the important role that blood plays in the "cleansing" process. Therefore, the only way that a spiritual "cleansing" can be achieved, is through a physical blood sacrifice, made on earth. The bible does not offer any alternative method.

With this puzzle solved, we will now determine what the word "sanctuary" means, when used in the religious context as: **"sanctuary be cleansed."**

In the "Old Testament" we discover that Solomon was commanded to build a temple: notice that this temple was also referred to as a **"sanctuary."**

> **"Take heed now; for the LORD hath chosen thee to build an house for the SANCTUARY: be strong, and do it"** (1 Chronicles 28:10).

When the word "sanctuary" was used, during "Old Testament" times, it often referred to a physical place on earth: like a tabernacle: or a temple: or another holy place, inside the temple, itself. We learn this from the following scriptures:

> **"And the TEMPLE and the SANCTUARY had two doors"** (Ezekiel 41:23).

> **"Yet they shall be ministers IN MY SANCTUARY, having charge at the gates of the house, and ministering to the house: they shall slay the burnt offering and the sacrifice for the people, and they shall stand before them to minister unto them"** (Ezekiel 44:11).

> **"The holy portion of the land shall be for the priests the ministers of the sanctuary, which shall come near to minister unto the Lord: and it shall be a place for their houses, and an HOLY PLACE FOR THE SANCTUARY"** (Ezekiel 25:4).

In fact, Moses was instructed to construct a portable tabernacle, during the Exodus, which was also referred to as "God's sanctuary."

> **"And let them MAKE ME A SANCTUARY; that I may dwell among them"** (Exodus 25:8).

In the next verse, we learn that God considered that "Solomon's Temple," was his house: "God's house."

> **"And he said unto me, Solomon thy son, he shall BUILD MY HOUSE and my courts: for I have chosen him to be my son, and I will be his father"** (1 Chronicles 28:6).

In the following scriptures, we learn that after Solomon built the temple, **"the glory of the Lord filled the house."** Notice that this temple was also referred to as **"the house of the Lord"** and **"the Lord's house:"**

> **"Now when Solomon had made an end of praying, the fire came down from heaven, and consumed the burnt offering and the sacrifices; and THE GLORY OF THE LORD FILLED THE HOUSE. And the priests could not enter into the house of the Lord, because the glory of the Lord had filled the LORD'S HOUSE"** (2 Chronicles 7:1-2).

Earlier, I mentioned that when Jesus bestowed the full authority of the Holy Priesthood upon the temple, in Jerusalem, that this is when the "Kingdom of God" was officially established, on earth, during that time. Therefore, when Daniel predicted that in 2300 years the "sanctuary" would be "cleansed," he was also predicting that another temple would have to be built, somewhere on earth, before this prophecy could be fulfilled. This is because the temple is the only place on earth, where the **"restitution of all things"** prophecies could begin to be fulfilled, and where the full authority of the Holy Priesthood could be restored, on earth, through the hands of Prophet Elijah. In fact, the "cleansing of the sanctuary" would be the last prophecy fulfilled, because this event would then "cleanse" and sanctify the official "Kingdom of God," on earth. However, none of these things would be possible, without the full authority of the Holy Priesthood, and this is what made the return of Prophet Elijah, during the "last days," so important.

Prophet Elijah

> "Behold, I will send you Elijah the prophet BEFORE the coming of the great and dreadful day of the Lord:" (Malachi 4:5).

THE FACT THAT Prophet Elijah was scheduled to arrive: **"before the coming of the great and dreadful day of the Lord,"** (before Jesus returns) proves that the fulfillment of this important prophecy, officially ushered in the "last days," on earth. This is when Prophet Elijah arrived in the temple, and bestowed the full authority of the Holy Priesthood, on earth. This when the "Kingdom of God" was officially established, on earth, and received the full authority of the Holy Priesthood, to carry out its assignments and duties.

> "Behold, I will send you Elijah the prophet before the coming of the great and dreadful day of the Lord: And he shall turn the heart of the fathers to the children, and the heart of the children to their fathers, LEST I COME AND SMITE THE EARTH WITH A CURSE" (Malachi 4:5-6).

However, it should also be noticed that these scriptures warn that the entire world will be smitten with a "curse," when Jesus arrives, if this holy ordinance is not strictly obeyed. This ordinance is being referred to, in these scriptures, as: **"he shall turn the heart of the fathers to the children, and the heart of the children to their fathers."** The fact that most modern-day ministers have no idea what this scripture is talking about, proves that they never received the authority, to perform this ordinance. Therefore, if obeying this scripture was their responsibility, the entire world would be smitten with a curse, when Jesus arrives.

In the following scripture, we learn that the temple played a very important role, before Jesus began his ministry:

> **"Behold, I will send my messenger, and he shall prepare the way before me: and the Lord, whom ye seek, shall suddenly come to his TEMPLE, even the messenger of the covenant, whom ye delight in: behold, he shall come, saith the Lord of hosts" (Malachi 3:1).**

This prophecy becomes easier to understand, after we add the missing names of the people, who fulfilled this prophecy:

> **"Behold, I will send my messenger (*"John the Baptist"*), and he shall prepare the way before me: and the Lord (*Jesus*), whom ye seek, shall suddenly come to his temple, even the messenger of the covenant (*Moses*), whom ye delight in: behold, he shall come, saith the Lord of hosts"** (Malachi 3:1).

This means that sometime before Jesus began his ministry, he met with "John the Baptist" and Moses, inside the temple. In fact, we learn from other scripture, that Jesus also met with Moses and Elias (Elijah), sometime later:

"And, behold, there appeared unto them Moses and Elias talking with him" (Matthew 17:3).

"And there appeared unto them Elias with Moses: and they were talking with Jesus" (Mark 9:4).

"And, behold, there talked with him two men, which were Moses and Elias" (Luke 9:30).

Note: the reference to "Elias" is completely misunderstood, in modern times, simply because "Elias" was often used as a priesthood title, which was given to certain individuals who were "called" (or chosen) to perform a specific priesthood duty: **"in the spirit and power of Elias."** Because "John the Baptist" was "called," to **"prepare ye the way of the Lord,"** is one example:

"And Jesus answered and said unto them, Elias truly shall first come, and restore all things. But I say unto you, That ELIAS IS COME ALREADY, and they knew him not, but have done unto him whatsoever they listed. Likewise shall also the Son of man suffer of them. Then the disciples understood that he spake unto them of John the Baptist" (Matthew 17:11-13).

In the following scripture, we learn that when Prophet Elijah returned, he was also performing his priesthood duty **"in the spirit and power of Elias:"**

"And he shall go before him IN THE SPIRIT AND POWER OF ELIAS, to turn the hearts of the fathers to the children, and the disobedient to the wisdom of the just; to make ready a people prepared for the Lord" (Luke 1:17).

The fact that Elijah performed his priesthood duty **"in the spirit and power of Elias,"** explains why he was also referred to as Elias, in the New Testament.

In the following scriptures, we learn that Elijah (Elias) and Moses met with Jesus, on the mount:

> **"And it came to pass about an eight days after these sayings, he took Peter and John and James, and went up into a mountain to pray. And as he prayed, the fashion of his countenance was altered, and his raiment was white and glistering. And, behold, there talked with him two men, which were MOSES AND ELIAS: Who appeared in glory, and spake of his decease which he should accomplish at Jerusalem"** (Luke 9:28-31).

To identify the "Elias," mentioned in this scripture, requires that we study about the "three-year drought," which Prophet Elijah placed upon the land:

> **"And ELIJAH the Tishbite, who was of the inhabitants of Gilead, said unto Ahab, As the Lord God of Israel liveth, before whom I stand, there shall not be dew nor rain these years, but according to my word"** (1 Kings 17:1).

We also learn, from the scriptures, that this draught lasted for three years:

> **"And it came to pass after many days, that the word of the Lord came to ELIJAH in the third year, saying, Go, shew thyself unto Ahab; and I will send rain upon the earth"** (1 Kings 18:1).

When this same event is explained, in the "New Testament," the name of "Elias" was substituted for the name of "Elijah."

> "**But I tell you of a truth, many widows were in Israel in the days of ELIAS, when the heaven was shut up three years and six months, when great famine was throughout all the land**" (Luke 4:25).

> "**ELIAS was a man subject to like passions as we are, and he prayed earnestly that it might not rain: and it rained not on the earth by the space of three years and six months**" (James 5:17).

In the following scripture we learn that Elijah **"let fire come down from heaven."**

> "**And ELIJAH answered and said to the captain of fifty, If I be a man of God, then let fire come down from heaven, and consume thee and thy fifty. And there came down fire from heaven, and consumed him and his fifty**" (2 Kings 1:10).

When this same event is mentioned, in the "New Testament," the name of "Elias" was once again substituted, for the name of "Elijah."

> "**And when his disciples James and John saw this, they said, Lord, wilt thou that we command fire to come down from heaven, and consume them, even as ELIAS did**" (Luke 9:54)?

These scriptures prove that Prophet Elijah was referred to as "Elias," many times, because he performed his priesthood duties: **"in the spirit and power of Elias."**

Because the temple is the only place on earth, where Prophet Elijah could "restore" the full authority of the Holy Priesthood, provides proof that another temple was built, before Elijah returned. The temple that fulfilled this prophecy, was dedicated on March 27, 1836, in Kirtland, Ohio. Prophet Elijah arrived in this temple, on April 3, 1836, which fulfilled the prophecy of Malachi (Malachi 4:5-6).

The Blood Sacrifice

To learn exactly how spiritual "cleansings" were performed, and why they were so important, requires that we fully understand the important role that blood would play in spiritual "cleansings." Earlier, we discussed that Moses sprinkled his book with a mixture of **"BLOOD from calves, goats, water, hyssop and scarlet wool."** It was the blood in this mixture, which spiritually "cleansed" and sanctified the words of Moses, and "sealed" his testimony, forever:

> **"For when Moses had spoken every precept to all the people according to the law, he took the blood of calves and of goats, with water, and scarlet wool, and hyssop, and sprinkled both the book, and all the people. Saying, This is the blood of the testament which God hath enjoined unto you. Moreover he sprinkled with blood both the tabernacle, and all the vessels of the ministry"** (Hebrews 9:19-21).

During "Old Testament" times, it was quite common for animals to be sacrificed, so their blood could be used to sanctify and seal the words of the prophets, and to "cleanse" the people from their sins. In the "New Testament" we are told that **"almost all things are by the law purged with blood."**

> "And almost all things are by the law purged with blood; and without shedding of blood is no remission" (Hebrews 9:22).

Therefore, this scripture proves that the only way to perform a spiritual "cleansing," is through a physical blood sacrifice, made on earth. The bible does not offer any alternative method.

In the following scriptures, we learn that Jesus introduced a "New Testament" on earth, when he proclaimed that his physical blood sacrifice had the power to save all mankind. Therefore, after Jesus was crucified, it was his physical blood sacrifice made on earth, which permanently abolished the daily animal blood sacrifices, for the remission of sins, from that time forward. It was also his physical blood sacrifice, which spiritually sanctified and "sealed" his testimony, forever.

> "For this is my blood of the NEW TESTAMENT, which is shed for many for the remission of sins" (Matthew 26:28).

> "And he said unto them, This is my blood of the NEW TESTAMENT, which is shed for many" (Mark 14:24).

> "Likewise also the cup after supper, saying, This cup is the NEW TESTAMENT in my blood, which is shed for you" (Luke 22:20).

> "After the same manner also he took the cup, when he had supped, saying, This cup is the NEW TESTAMENT in my blood: this do ye, as oft as ye drink it, in remembrance of me" (1 Corinthians 11:25).

In the following scripture, we learn that Jesus was required to die, so that his "New Testament" would be placed in force:

> "For where a testament is, there must also of necessity be the death of the testator. For a testament is of force after men are dead: otherwise it is of no strength at all while the testator liveth" (Hebrews 9:16-17).

Therefore, because the "New Testament" that Jesus introduced, was officially placed in force after he was crucified, explains why **"the blood of Jesus Christ"** "cleanseth" us from our sins, today:

> **"But if we walk in the light, as he is in the light, we have fellowship one with another, and THE BLOOD OF JESUS CHRIST HIS SON CLEANSETH US FROM ALL SIN"** (1 John 1:7).

These scriptures prove that every individual, who introduces a "new testament" on earth, would be required to die. It would be through his physical blood sacrifice, made on earth, which would spiritually "cleanse" and sanctify his "new testament," and "seal" his testimony, forever:

> **"For where a testament is, there must also of necessity be the death of the testator. For a testament is of force after men are dead: otherwise it is of no strength at all while the testator liveth"** (Hebrews 9:16-17).

In order to qualify as a "new testament," requires that this "new testament" must be completely different, from what we already have in our possession. In other words, because we already have the Holy Bible in our possession, proves that another bible version would not qualify as a "new testament."

In the following scripture, we learn that blood sacrifices were sometimes made **"for the kingdom,"** itself:

> **"And they brought seven bullocks, and seven rams, and seven lambs, and seven he goats, for a sin offering for the kingdom, and for the sanctuary, and for Judah. And he commanded the priests the sons of Aaron to offer them on the altar of the Lord"** (2 Chronicles 29:21).

Understand; after the people in Judah, turned their backs on God, they began to worship many different false gods, and idols. As a result, everything that these people touched was considered "unclean," which included the temple, itself. Therefore, after King Hezekiah restored the worship of Jehovah, throughout his kingdom, it was necessary to perform several blood sacrifices, to spiritually "cleanse" his kingdom," the "sanctuary," and Judah. We learn, from this scripture, that it took a total of 28 animals to perform these spiritual "cleansings."

What Happened in 1844

We learn from the following scriptures that Daniel's "sanctuary be cleansed" prophecy was scheduled to be fulfilled, in 2300 days (years), from some unspecified date:

> "Then I heard one saint speaking, and another saint said unto that certain saint which spake, How long shall be the vision concerning the daily sacrifice, and the transgression of desolation, to give both the sanctuary and the host to be trodden under foot? And he said unto me, UNTO TWO THOUSAND AND THREE HUNDRED DAYS; THEN SHALL THE SANCTUARY BE CLEANSED" (Daniel 8:13-14).

Here is how to calculate exactly when this prophecy was scheduled to be fulfilled:

Earlier, we talked about the **"edict to restore"** document, which was officially placed in force, in 457 B.C. (Ezra 8). This is the year that we will now use to solve this prophecy. Therefore, when we calculate forward 2300 years from 457 B.C. (or subtract 457 B.C. from 2300), we end up with 1843. Because we are calculating from B.C. to A.D., we must not forget to add the one missing zero-year, to match our modern-day calendar. This converts 1843 to 1844. As you can see, these calculations prove that the "sanctuary be cleansed" prophecy was scheduled to be fulfilled, sometime in 1844. Because every bible prophecy will be fulfilled, **on earth**, without exception, proves that this prophecy was also fulfilled on earth. Besides, why would Christians need to know about a prophecy, which could never be proven fulfilled or not? What good would a prophecy of this kind be to anyone? The fact that this prophecy was fulfilled, **on earth**, sometime in 1844, proves that this prophecy was fulfilled in a completely different manner, then what many ministers expected. Therefore, when we compare this prophecy with the historical record, we learn exactly when and how this "sanctuary be cleansed" prophecy was fulfilled.

Therefore, Daniel was simply predicting that sometime during the "last days," a physical blood sacrifice would be made, ***on earth***, which would spiritually "cleanse" and sanctify the official "Kingdom of God," on earth. The fact that blood does not exist in heaven, provides proof that this prophecy was fulfilled on earth, right on schedule.

> **"Now this I say, brethren, that flesh and BLOOD cannot inherit the kingdom of God; neither doth corruption inherit incorruption"** (1 Corinthians 15:50).

Because so many ministers expected that Jesus was returning to earth, in 1844, provides proof that they were not closely watching any events unfolding on earth, during that time. As a result, they failed to recognize the event that fulfilled this prophecy, on earth, even though it was widely reported in the media. When we compare Daniel's "sanctuary be cleansed" prophecy, with the historical record, we learn that it was Prophet Joseph Smith who fulfilled this prophecy, when he was martyred in Carthage, Illinois on **June 27, 1844**. In other words, the blood sacrifice of Prophet Joseph Smith, not only spiritually "cleansed" God's "sanctuary," and officially established that "The Church of Jesus Christ of Latter-day Saints" is the official "Kingdom of God" on earth today, but it also "sealed" his testimony, forever. The fact that "The Church of Jesus Christ of Latter-day Saints" was established on earth, during the reign of the "ten kings," and that Prophet Joseph Smith was martyred in 1844, provides proof that God's True Church exists on earth, today. Only One Church on earth fulfilled these prophecies.

I realize that most modern-day Christians will have a difficult time, accepting the fact that Joseph Smith was a true prophet, of God. Therefore, most Christians will probably be shocked when they learn, that Aaron also had some doubts, concerning his brother Moses. Understand; Aaron's skepticism about Moses, raised its ugly head, long after the miracles were performed in Egypt, which forced the Pharaoh to release the Israelites from his captivity (Exodus 8). We learn about Aaron's skepticism, in the "Book of Numbers," when Aaron discusses his concerns, with his sister Miriam:

> **"And Miriam and Aaron spake against Moses because of the Ethiopian woman whom he had married: for he had married an Ethiopian woman. (Now the man Moses was very meek, above all the men which were upon the face of the earth.) And the LORD spake suddenly unto Moses, and unto Aaron, and unto Miriam, Come out ye three unto the tabernacle of the congregation. And they three came out. And the LORD came down in the pillar of the cloud, and stood in the door of the tabernacle, and called Aaron and Miriam: and they both came forth. And he said, Hear now my words: IF THERE BE A PROPHET AMONG YOU, I THE LORD WILL MAKE MYSELF KNOWN UNTO HIM IN A VISION, AND WILL SPEAK UNTO HIM IN A DREAM. My servant Moses is not so, who is faithful in all mine house. With him will I speak mouth to mouth, even apparently, and not in dark speeches;**

and the similitude of the LORD shall he behold: wherefore then were ye not afraid to speak against my servant Moses?" (Numbers: 12:1-7).

In the next verse, we learn that God became very angry toward Aaron and Miriam, because they spoke against Moses:

Numbers 12:8, "And the anger of the LORD was kindled against them; and he departed."

When studying these scriptures, it needs to be remembered that God also made a very important promise, in verse six, when he proclaimed: **"If there be a prophet among you, I the LORD will make myself known unto him in a vision, and will speak unto him in a dream."** In other words, God is simply explaining how to recognize a true prophet, from the many false prophets that exist, in modern times. This is because God promised that he would personally visit his chosen prophet, in a vision, and would speak with him in a dream (Numbers 12:6).

For over 180 years, many ministers have accused Prophet Joseph Smith, of being a false prophet. However, it seems that these ministers never compared the testimony of Prophet Joseph Smith, with the promise that God made, in this scripture (Numbers 12:6).

When studying the historical record, we learn that Prophet Joseph Smith testified many times, that "God the Father" and his son "Jesus Christ," appeared to him in a vision. This event occurred in 1820, when Joseph Smith began to pray for help, so that he could decide which denomination to join. It was during this prayer, when two personages suddenly appeared, and when one spoke the following words: **"This is my beloved Son. Hear Him!"**

Here is the testimony of Prophet Joseph Smith:

> "My object in going to inquire of the Lord was to know which of all the sects was right, that I might know which to join. No sooner, therefore, did I get possession of myself, so as to be able to speak, than I asked the Personages who stood above me in the light, which of all the sects was right (for at this time it had never entered into my heart that all were wrong)—and which I should join. I was answered that I must join none of them, for they were all wrong; and the Personage who addressed me said that all their creeds were an abomination in his sight; that those professors were all corrupt; that: they draw near to me with their lips, but their hearts are far from me, they teach for doctrines the commandments of men, having a form of godliness, but they deny the power thereof" (Joseph Smith History 1:18-19).

Notice that this vision fulfilled the promise, which God made, when he declared: **"I the LORD will make myself known unto him in a vision"** (Numbers 12:5). Therefore, because Prophet Joseph Smith passes this test, provides more proof that he was a true prophet of God.

In case you still have some doubt, concerning the truthfulness for "The Church of Jesus Christ of Latter-day Saints," then here is another prophecy that this church fulfilled:

> "And it shall come to pass IN THE LAST DAYS, that the mountain of the Lord's house shall be established in the top of the mountains, and shall be exalted above the hills; and all nations shall flow unto it" (Isaiah 2:2).

> "But IN THE LAST DAYS it shall come to pass, that the

mountain of the house of the Lord shall be established in the top of the mountains, and it shall be exalted above the hills; and people shall flow unto it" (Micah 4:1).

Therefore, is it only by coincidence that the headquarters for "The Church of Jesus Christ of Latter-day Saints," was established in the very **top of the Rocky Mountains?** Is it also by coincidence that many people from all over the world, visit the Salt Lake City Temple, every year? Even though Utah has several beautiful National Parks, the temple is the most visited attraction in the state of Utah, which is fulfilling the "latter-day" prophecy: **"and all nations shall flow unto it,"** and **"people shall flow unto it."** This provides more proof that "The Church of Jesus Christ of Latter-day Saints" is the restored "Kingdom of God," on earth, today. In fact, this is the only church, which fulfilled the bible prophecies that we discussed. No other church, on earth, has ever claimed that they fulfilled these prophecies.

The "Restitution of all Things"

Earlier, we discussed how Isaiah's prophecy: **"And the Gentiles shall come to the light, and the kings to the brightness of thy rising"** (Isaiah 60:3) was fulfilled, between the years of 1806 and 1848. This is when the true Church of Jesus Christ was established, on earth, and when the **"restitution of all things"** prophecy (Acts 3:21) began to be fulfilled. Isaiah, Ezekiel, and "John the Revelator" talked about a "sealed" book (a "little book"), which would make its appearance on earth, sometime during the last days. To fully understand the important role that this "sealed" book" would play, in fulfilling the **"restitution of all things"** prophecy, requires that we begin our discussion with the "Book of Isaiah," chapter twenty-nine. To make this chapter easier to understand, a verse by verse interpretation, is also provided. Study this interpretation, and then decide (for yourself), if the correct interpretation was achieved, or not.

Isaiah Chapter 29
King James Version

Isaiah 29:1, "Woe to Ariel, to Ariel, the city where David dwelt! add ye year to year; let them kill sacrifices."

INTERPRETATION: THIS WAS a warning given to Ariel (another name for Jerusalem), about the destruction that it would face, sometime in the future (the future from Isaiah's perspective). The phrase: **"add ye year to year; let them kill sacrifices,"** is referring to the daily blood sacrifices, which were performed daily for the remission of sins. Also notice that the name Ariel was mentioned twice. Isaiah was simply warning the Israelites, that the temple in Jerusalem would be destroyed, at two different times. The first destruction occurred in 587 B.C., through the hands of King Nebuchadnezzar, while the second destruction was carried out by the Romans, in 70 A.D.

Isaiah 29:2, "Yet I will distress Ariel, and there shall be heaviness and sorrow: and it shall be unto me as Ariel."

Interpretation: this verse is explaining how the people in Judah and Israel, will feel, after the temple in Jerusalem is destroyed. But then Isaiah adds another hidden message: **"and it shall be UNTO ME AS**

ARIEL." Meaning: that this same thing will happen to someone else, sometime in the future, *after* Jerusalem is destroyed in 70 A.D. It is very important to understand that not only was Jerusalem destroyed, in 70 A.D., but the people were also removed from their lands.

Isaiah 29:3, "And I will camp against thee round about, and will lay siege against thee with a mount, and I will raise forts against thee."

Interpretation: Isaiah then explains how this different group of people will be conquered. Understand; this verse is not talking about the people in Jerusalem, Judah, or Israel. This is because this prophecy was not even scheduled to be fulfilled, until sometime after Jerusalem is destroyed, in 70 A.D. Isaiah is explaining how this same destruction will happen, to a completely different group of people, sometime after 70 A.D.

Isaiah 29:4, "And thou shalt be brought down, and shalt speak out of the ground, and thy speech shall be low out of the dust, and thy voice shall be, as of one that hath a familiar spirit, out of the ground, and thy speech shall whisper out of the dust."

Interpretation: Isaiah explains that these people will be defeated: **"and thou shalt be brought down."** However, he then adds another mysterious message: **"their voices will whisper out of the dust."** The only way for this prophecy to be fulfilled: **"their voices will whisper out of the dust,"** is for a written record of these people, to be discovered. By what other means would it be possible for their voices to **"whisper out of the dust?"**

Isaiah 29:5, "Moreover the multitude of thy strangers shall be like small dust, and the multitude of the terrible ones shall be

as chaff that passeth away: yea, it shall be at an instant suddenly."
Interpretation: Isaiah continues to explain that many **"strangers"** will take over their land: **"multitude of thy strangers shall be like small dust."** Notice that he uses the phrase: **"the terrible ones,"** and predicts that they **"shall be as chaff that passeth away,"** which simply means that after these people are defeated, they will be forgotten. This prophecy is talking about the European settlers (**"thy strangers"**) who colonized the American continent. These early settlers would often complain that the Native Americans were a terrible enemy to fight (**"the terrible ones"**), because of the terrible tactics that they often used, against their enemies. This verse is comparing the Native Americans, with the **"chaff"** (the grain husks), which is separated from the wheat and cast away: **"And the multitude of the terrible ones shall be as chaff that passeth away."** This means that after the Native Americans are defeated, they will then be cast to the side, and forgotten. It needs to be understood, from the historical perspective, that this prophecy was fulfilled in a very short time: **"yea, it shall be at an instant suddenly."**

Isaiah 29:6, "Thou shalt be visited of the Lord of hosts with thunder, and with earthquake, and great noise, with storm and tempest, and the flame of devouring fire."

Interpretation: Isaiah then explains how this destruction will be carried out. To fully comprehend what Isaiah is talking about, it needs to be understood what would happen if the **"Lord of hosts"** visited **"with thunder, and with earthquake, and great noise, with storm and tempest, and the flame of devouring fire."** Anyone who would face such an arsenal, from the Lord of hosts, would be completely wiped out.

Isaiah 29:7, "And the multitude of all the nations that fight against Ariel, even all that fight against her and her

munition, and that distress her, shall be as a dream of a night vision."

Interpretation: Isaiah suddenly switches gears and begins talking about the "last days." He is explaining that anyone who dares fight against Ariel (Jerusalem and modern-day Israel), will be destroyed by God, and will only be remembered like a dream: **"as a dream of a night vision."** Understand; if this promise was in effect before 70 A.D., Jerusalem would not have been destroyed by the Romans, and the temple would still be standing, today. Therefore, it needs to be understood that Israel did not receive this protection, until sometime *after* Jerusalem was destroyed, in 70 A.D. In other words, this protection was scheduled to go into effect, after the people of Israel return to their homeland, during the "last days." Therefore, this promise is in full force, today, and any nation that dares to fight against Israel will be defeated.

Isaiah 29:8, "It shall even be as when an hungry man dreameth, and, behold, he eateth; but he awaketh, and his soul is empty: or as when a thirsty man dreameth, and, behold, he drinketh; but he awaketh, and, behold, he is faint, and his soul hath appetite: so shall the multitude of all the nations be, that fight against mount Zion."

Interpretation: Isaiah continues to explain what will happen, to the nations, who decide to fight against Israel, during the "last days." Notice that this protection was also extended to mount Zion: **"so shall the multitude of all the nations be, that fight against mount Zion.**

Question: why would it be necessary, for this protection to be extended to mount Zion, if mount Zion is in Israel?

This particular "mount Zion" is referring to the "Kingdom of God" (God's True Church), which was scheduled to be established, on earth, sometime during the "last days." Therefore, according to this prophecy, the true Church of Jesus Christ will also be protected from destruction.

Isaiah 29:9, "Stay yourselves, and wonder; cry ye out, and cry: they are drunken, but not with wine; they stagger, but not with strong drink."

Interpretation: the word "drunkenness" is another term, for the people in apostasy, who are not living their lives on the straight and narrow path. These people are staggering around, in their lives, as if they are drunk. Be aware that this warning applies to everyone, reading this verse, at this very moment. Therefore, *we* are being warned to be on **our** guard (**"stay yourselves"**), so that *we* do not get caught up in the same predicament. This means that *we* must strictly obey God's laws, and commandments, and begin to live **our** lives on the straight and narrow path; so that *we* do not stagger around, in **our** lives, as if **we** are drunk.

Isaiah 29:10, "For the Lord hath poured out upon you the spirit of deep sleep, and hath closed your eyes: the prophets and your rulers, the seers hath he covered."

Interpretation: when this verse says: **"the Lord hath poured out upon you the spirit of deep sleep, and hath closed your eyes,"** Isaiah is talking about the worldwide apostasy (the spiritual darkness), which began to spread around the world, shortly after the temple in Jerusalem was destroyed, in 70 A.D. This is when direct communication between God, and his chosen prophets (and seers), was suspended for many centuries: **"the prophets and your rulers, the seers hath he covered."** This verse confirms what we previously discussed, concerning the prophecy: **"Let no man deceive you by any means: for that day shall not come except there come a falling away first"** (2 Thessalonians 2:3-4). A "falling away" is referring to the apostasy, while the phrase:

"for that day shall not come," is talking about the return of Jesus. In other words, Isaiah is warning that there will be a time when God will not speak to the people, through his chosen prophets, and seers. This "falling away" (apostasy) began to spread around the world, shortly after 70 A.D., just like Amos predicted (Amos 8).

Isaiah 29:11, "And the vision of all is become unto you as the words of a book that is sealed, which men deliver to one that is learned, saying, Read this, I pray thee: and he saith, I cannot; for it is sealed:"

Interpretation: sometime after the apostasy (spiritual darkness) covers the entire world, is when a "sealed" book will make its appearance, on earth: **"and the vision of all is become unto you as the words of a book that is sealed, which men deliver to one that is learned, saying Read this, I pray thee: and he saith, I cannot; for it is sealed."** The reason why this book is "sealed," is because it was written in an unknown language (or a lost language), which would have to be translated ("unsealed") before it could be introduced into the world. Many modern-day scholars have erroneously assumed that this verse is possibly talking about the "Holy Bible." However, it needs to be understood that the Holy Bible never arrived on the scene, as a "sealed" book. The bible is simply a compilation of many ancient letters and manuscripts, written by the early prophets, which were later gathered up to create a book. Therefore, the Holy Bible never arrived on the scene, in an unknown language (or a lost language), which had to be translated before it could be introduced into the world. Even though many of the letters, and manuscripts were written in different languages, these languages were known, which proves that the Holy Bible, itself, never arrived on the scene as a "sealed" book.

Note: even though some bible prophecies were "sealed," until after the "last days" arrived, does not prove that the entire bible was "sealed." If the Holy Bible was "sealed," we would not be able to read its scriptures, until after the Holy Bible is "unsealed."

This is now the perfect time, to bring the "Book of Revelation" into this discussion, which provides an accurate timetable, for exactly when this mysterious "sealed" book was scheduled to arrive on earth:

> **"But in the days of the voice of the seventh angel, when he shall begin to sound, the mystery of God should be finished, as he hath declared to his servants the prophets"** (Revelation 10:7).

Interpretation: when this verse proclaims: **"But in the days of the voice of the seventh angel, when he shall begin to sound,"** is creating a timetable. **"The days of the seventh angel,"** is referring to the seventh thousandth year, when the **"voice of the seventh angel"** will **"begin to sound."** Therefore, after a total of six thousand years have passed, Jesus will then return to earth, which is when: **"the mystery of God should be finished, as he hath declared to his servants the prophets."** The six thousand years are calculated from the fall of Adam. However, it should also be remembered that this scheduled time period was also predicted to be shortened, as explained by Matthew and Mark (Matthew 24:22; Mark 13:20). As a result, this means that the **"voice of the seventh angel"** could actually **"begin to sound,"** at any time. Therefore, because we are living on earth, during the sixth thousandth year, provides proof that this mysterious "sealed" book (Isaiah 29:11), would already exist on earth. To learn more, about this "sealed" book, we will now continue:

> **"And the voice which I heard from heaven spake unto me again, and said, go and take THE LITTLE BOOK which is open in the HAND OF THE ANGEL which standeth upon the sea and upon the earth"** (Revelation 10:8).

Interpretation: notice that John was instructed to **"go and take the little book which is open in the hand of the ANGEL, which STANDETH UPON THE SEA AND UPON THE EARTH."** We learn from this verse, that John sees a little book, which was opened in the hands of an ANGEL. Also notice that this angel is standing upon the sea, and upon the earth, and not just standing on dry land. This symbolism is very important, because it reveals that this little book was not written in Israel, or anywhere within the Middle Eastern countries. Because we see this angel standing on both the sea, and the earth, provides proof that this "little book" was written in another part of the world: across the sea from Israel and the Middle East. The fact that this "little book" was not written, in the Middle East, provides more proof that this prophecy is not talking about the Holy Bible. The only way for the Holy Bible to be connected, to this prophecy, would require that this angel be standing on dry land with both feet. The fact that we see this angel standing on the sea, and the earth, implies that this "little book" will be written, across the sea from Israel.

"And I went unto the angel, and said unto him, Give me the little book. And he said unto me, Take it, and eat it up; and it shall make thy belly bitter, but it shall be in thy mouth sweet as honey. And I took the little book out of the angel's hand, and ate it up; and it was in my mouth sweet as honey: and as soon as I had eaten it, my belly was bitter" (Revelation 10:9-10).

Interpretation: John then takes this "little book," from the hands of the angel, and eats it up. Because this book was as "sweet as honey" in his mouth, was a sign given to John, that this "little book" contains the "words of God." This is because the "words of God" are as sweet, as honey, as explained in the following scriptures:

"The fear of the Lord is clean, enduring forever: the

judgments of the Lord are true and righteous altogether. More to be desired are they than gold, yea, than much fine gold: SWEETER ALSO THAN HONEY AND THE HONEYCOMB" (Psalms 19:9-10).

"How sweet are thy words unto my taste! yea, SWEETER THAN HONEY TO MY MOUTH" (Psalms 119:103).

When this "little book" became bitter in John's belly, it was a sign given to John, that he was *not* the person who was "chosen" to introduce this "little book" into the world. Notice that this also eliminates the "Book of Revelation," from this prophecy, because John wrote the "Book of Revelation," which also means that he introduced this book into the world. Therefore, in accordance with this prophecy, if John had eaten the "Book of Revelation," it would have tasted "sweet as honey" in his mouth, and would have remained "sweet as honey," in his belly. The fact that this "little book" became "bitter," proves that John was **not** the person who was "chosen" to introduce this "little book," into the world.

"And he said unto me, Thou must prophesy again before many peoples, and nations, and tongues, and kings" (Revelation 10:11).

Interpretation: even though John was not "chosen," to bring forth this "little book," he was informed that he would perform another important duty: **"Thou must prophesy AGAIN before many peoples and nations, and tongues and kings."** This means that John would prophecy again, on earth, sometime after his death: after he becomes a resurrected being. What many scholars have often overlooked, concerning this prophecy, is the fact that Jesus and his disciples talked about this promise, earlier (see John 21:21-23).

Verse 21, "Peter seeing him saith to Jesus, Lord, and what shall this man do?"

Verse 22, "Jesus saith unto him, If I will that he tarry till I come, what is that to thee? follow thou me."

Verse 23, "Then went this saying abroad among the brethren, that that disciple should not die: yet Jesus said not unto him, He shall not die; but, If I will that he tarry till I come, what is that to thee?"

These scriptures prove that Jesus, and his disciples, discussed the promise that Jesus gave to John. However, because Peter did not fully understand this promise, he then asked Jesus the following question (verse 21): **"and what shall this man do?"** In verse twenty-three, we learn that the brethren (the disciples) had mistakenly assumed that Jesus promised John, that he would not die. But Jesus explains that this was not the promise that he gave to John, at all: **"Jesus said not unto him, He shall not die."** Jesus then explains that John would be allowed to tarry, on earth, until Jesus returns: **"tarry till I come."** Jesus then responds, to his disciples, with the following question: **"If I will"** (if I decide) **"that he"** (John) should **"tarry till I come"** (remain on earth until I return) **"what is that to thee?"** Therefore, the promise that John received from Jesus, would allow John to return to earth after he dies, and remain on earth (tarry) until Jesus returns. John would then return to earth, as a resurrected being, and prophesy again. Even though John received this promise from Jesus, it needs to be remembered that John was not the person who was "chosen," to introduce the **"little book"** into the world. This "little book" was scheduled to arrive on earth, through the hands of an angel, which would then be delivered into the hands of another chosen servant, many centuries after the death of John.

We will now leave the "Book of Revelation," and continue this research with the "Book of Ezekiel," so that we can learn more about this mysterious "sealed" book (Ezekiel 37:16-19). However, before we begin, there are a few things that we need to discuss. After the ancient books were written, they were often rolled up on sticks, or scrolls. Therefore, if you wanted to know how many books that you had, in your possession, you would simply count the sticks: 10 sticks would equal 10 books. Another thing to remember is that some of these books were named after the different tribes of Israel. For example: the correct title for the "Holy Bible" should be the "Book of Judah." This is because the bible was written for the "House of Judah," which would then be shared with the other tribes, of Israel. Ezekiel talks about another book, which would be written, for the "House of Ephraim." Two different books, named after two different tribes, of Israel. It needs to be remembered that when Jacob (Israel) blessed Joseph's sons (Ephraim and Manasseh), he gave the greater blessing to Ephraim, and his descendants (Genesis 48:16-20). This meant that the "House of Ephraim" would eventually become a multitude of nations. Therefore, any book that would come forth, from the "House of Ephraim," would help fulfill this promise. With this understanding we will now continue:

"Moreover, thou son of man, take thee one stick, and write upon it, For Judah, and for the children of Israel his companions: then take another stick, and write upon it, For Joseph, the stick of Ephraim, and [for] all the house of Israel his companions" (Ezekiel 37:16).

Interpretation: this verse is talking about writing upon two different sticks (two different books or scrolls): one stick is for **"Judah,"** while the other stick is for **"Joseph, the stick of Ephraim."** It needs to be understood that the "Old and New Testaments" together, were written for the "House of Judah," which would also be shared with the other tribes of Israel. In accordance with this prophecy, another book would be written for the "House of Ephraim," which would also be shared with the other tribes of Israel. Is it possible that this second book would exist, on earth, today?

"And join them one to another into one stick; and they shall become one in thine hand" (Ezekiel 37:17).

Interpretation: notice that Ezekiel predicts that these two "sticks" (both books) will be seen, together, and will become as one book in thy hand: **"one in thine hand."** In other words, both books will contain the "words of God," and both books will be taught together, as one book. It would not be possible for both books, to become **"one in thine hand,"** if both books do not contain the "words of God."

"Say unto them, Thus saith the Lord GOD; Behold, I will take the stick of Joseph, which is in the hand of Ephraim, and the tribes of Israel his fellows, and will put them with him, even with the stick of Judah, and make them one stick, and they shall be one in mine hand" (Ezekiel 37:19).

Interpretation: this prophecy continues to explain that both books will be seen together, and will become as one book, in God's hands: **"one in mine hand."** Once again, this proves that both books, contain the "words of God."

"And the sticks whereon thou writest shall be in thine hand before their eyes" (Ezekiel 37:20).

Interpretation: this verse confirms, that both books will be seen, together: **"in thine hand before their eyes."**

Note: it needs to be understood that the "Old and New Testaments" are not considered, two separate books, written for two different tribes of Israel. In accordance with Ezekiel's prophecies, the entire "Holy Bible" was written for the "House of Judah," which would then be shared with the other tribes of Israel (Ezekiel 37:16). We also learn that a second book will be written for the "House of Ephraim." This second book will also be shared with the other tribes of Israel (Ezekiel 37:16). The fact that the "House of Judah," and the "House of Ephraim" are two separate tribes, proves that this second book will be separate from the Holy Bible.

We will now return to the "Book of Isaiah," to see if we can uncover any more clues, concerning this mysterious "sealed" book:

Isaiah 29:11, "And the vision of all is become unto you as the words of a book that is sealed, which men deliver to one that is learned, saying, Read this, I pray thee: and he saith, I cannot; for it is sealed:"

Interpretation: we learn from this prophecy, that this "sealed" book will be given into the hands of a *learned* man, or an educated man, who will then proclaim that he cannot read a "sealed" book. The reason why this book is still "sealed," during that time, is because this book was written in an unknown language, which the learned man could not translate. Once again, this proves that this "sealed" book was not the Holy Bible, because the bible was never written in an unknown language, or a lost language.

Isaiah 29:12, "And the book is delivered to him that is not learned, saying, Read this, I pray thee: and he saith, I am not learned."

Interpretation: this "sealed" book is then delivered to an uneducated man: **"and he saith, I am not learned."** Even though the educated man could not read this "sealed" book, the uneducated man successfully "unsealed" this book, when he translated this book from its "unknown" language.

> **Isaiah 29:13, "Wherefore the Lord said, Forasmuch as this people draw near me with their mouth, and with their lips do honour me, but have removed their heart far from me, and their fear toward me is taught by the precept of men:"**

Interpretation: this verse is talking about the modern-day Christians, who only worship God with the lips, but fail to strictly obey God's commandments, to the best of their ability: **"but have removed their heart far from me."** Many modern-day Christians will often profess that they believe in God, but very few will choose to change their lives, and strictly obey God's laws and commandments, to the best of their ability. Because so many ministers fail to understand what it really means, to **"fear God,"** they created a false doctrine: **"their FEAR toward me is taught by the PRECEPT OF MEN."** To **"fear God"** means to obey God, and to worship him, but it does not mean that we should be afraid of our Heavenly Father. In my opinion, the "Book of Proverbs," explains this best:

> **"My son, if thou wilt receive my words, and hide my commandments with thee; so that thou incline thine ear unto wisdom, and apply thine heart to understanding; yea, if thou criest after knowledge, and liftest up thy voice for understanding; if thou seekest her as silver, and searchest for her as for hid treasures; then shalt thou understand the fear of the Lord, and find the knowledge of God. For the Lord giveth wisdom: out of his mouth cometh knowledge and understanding"** (Proverbs 2:1-6).

Therefore, when you obey God's commandments, and search the scriptures for more knowledge and understanding, you will gradually begin to understand the true meaning behind the words: **"to fear the Lord."** Does any of this sound like that we should fear (or be afraid) of our Heavenly Father? To **"fear God,"** simply means to worship God, and to put our faith in God, and to obey him to the best of our ability, which will then prove (to God) that we are worthy.

> **Isaiah 29:14, "Therefore, behold, I will proceed to do a marvellous work among this people, even a marvellous work and a wonder: for the wisdom of their wise men shall perish, and the understanding of their prudent men shall be hid."**

Interpretation: sometime during the time, when most Christians will only worship God with their lips, is when God will perform a **"marvelous work and a wonder."** This is when this "sealed" book will arrive, on earth, to be "unsealed." This book will teach the truth, in such a manner, that **"the wisdom of their wise men shall perish, and the understanding of their prudent men shall be hid."** The term **"wise men"** is referring to the ministers and priests. The term **"prudent men"** is referring to the bible scholars and theologians. Therefore, this "unsealed" book will prove that the **"wise men"** are "unwise," and that many of the doctrines created by the **"prudent men,"** are false.

> **Isaiah 29:15, "Woe unto them that seek deep to hide their counsel from the LORD, and their works are in the dark, and they say, Who seeth us? and who knoweth us?"**

Interpretation: this verse is speaking directly to the modern-day ministers and priests, who believe that they can hide their true motives, from God.

> **Isaiah 29:16, "Surely your turning of things upside down shall be esteemed as the potter's clay: for shall the work say**

of him that made it, He made me not? or shall the thing framed say of him that framed it, He had no understanding?"

Interpretation: Isaiah then explains that most ministers have turned the "words of God" upside down: **"Surely your turning of things upside down shall be esteemed as the potter's clay."** Even though this "unsealed" book will arrive on earth, through the hands of an angel, and through the hands of God's chosen messenger, many ministers will continue to say that this "unsealed" book is false: and that this "little book" does not contain the "words of God." This verse is comparing their false accusations, with potter's clay and a picture frame, by asking the following questions: would the work of the potter turn to the potter and then say: **"he made me not?"** Would the frame turn to the framer and then say: **"he doesn't understand what he's doing?"** In other words, even though this "unsealed" book will arrive on earth, in the same manner that God used many times in the past, most ministers and priests will still reject the words written in this "little book."

Isaiah 29:17, "Is it not yet a very little while, and Lebanon shall be turned into a fruitful field, and the fruitful field shall be esteemed as a forest?"

This verse is creating an accurate timetable, which proves that this "unsealed" book would arrive, on earth, during the "last days." However, before we can fully understand this prophecy, there are few things that we need to learn about Lebanon. Lebanon was ruled by the Ottoman Empire, for many centuries, and its territory was established within the mountainous regions, surrounding the Lebanon Mountains. In 1918, after World War I, these territorial boundaries were extended from the valley behind the mountains, all the way to the seacoast. This was done so that Lebanon could have a seaport of its own. During biblical times, the Lebanon Mountains were well known for its beautiful forests of Lebanon Cedars, which many historians claim was used to build

Solomon's temple. In fact, this tree is proudly displayed on the modern Lebanese flag, today. Because Lebanon is located, within the corn-belt region of the earth, means that a large portion of its fertile fields are planted with corn: **"fruitful field."** Even though the Lebanon Cedars still exist, today, they are not as abundant as they once flourished, during biblical times. This is because it takes a minimum of one thousand years for these trees to grow to maturity. With this information, we are now ready to decipher, the following prophecy (Isaiah 29:17).

Isaiah 29:17, "Is it not yet a very little while, and Lebanon shall be turned into a fruitful field, and the fruitful field shall be esteemed as a forest?"

Interpretation: the phrase: **"Is it not yet a very little while, and Lebanon shall be turned into a fruitful field"** is referring to the time when the boundaries for modern-day Lebanon, are extended to the seacoast. In other words, shortly after this "unsealed" book arrives on earth, the boundaries for modern-day Lebanon will be extended, which will give the people of Lebanon their fertile fields, that they will plant with corn: **"and Lebanon shall be turned into a fruitful field."** This verse then asks this question: "will the people of Lebanon esteem (admire) their "fruitful fields," as much as they do, their beautiful forests of cedar trees?" Meaning of: **"the fruitful field shall be esteemed as a forest?"** This timetable is important to understand, because it reveals that this "unsealed" book was scheduled to arrive on earth, slightly before the territory boundaries for modern-day Lebanon are extended to the seacoast. The fact that these boundaries were changed in 1918, proves that this book arrived, slightly before 1918. In fact, the reference to the "fruitful field" provides proof, that this prophecy is not talking about some ancient territorial boundary. Because the Holy Bible existed, many centuries before the boundaries for modern-day Lebanon were extended, also proves that this prophecy is not talking about the Holy Bible.

Isaiah 29:18, "And in that day shall the deaf hear the words of the book, and the eyes of the blind shall see out of obscurity, and out of darkness."

Interpretation: **"And in that day"** (slightly before the boundaries of Lebanon are extended) **"shall the deaf"** (referring to the people in apostasy) will **"hear the words of the book."** Also notice that the **"eyes of the blind"** (referring to the people in apostasy) **"shall see out of obscurity, and out of darkness."** It needs to be understood that the people in apostasy are often referred to as the people who "cannot see and hear." We learn this from the "Book of Romans," when it proclaims: **"According as it is written, God hath given them the spirit of slumber, eyes that they should not see, and ears, that they should not hear"** (Romans 11:8). We learn from Isaiah that after this "unsealed" book arrives, it will have the power to remove the apostasy, from earth. This is when the people, who read this book **"shall see out of obscurity, and out of darkness,"** and will no longer be in "spiritual darkness."

Isaiah 29:19, "The meek also shall increase their joy in the LORD, and the poor among men shall rejoice in the Holy One of Israel."

Interpretation: this verse is explaining that the meek and the poor, will also rejoice in Jesus Christ, and will recognize Jesus as the "Holy One of Israel." It is interesting to note that the "Holy One of Israel" is mentioned in the "Old Testament," a total of fifty-one times, but not mentioned once in the "New Testament." Therefore, the "New Testament" never explains that Jesus is the "Holy One of Israel." However, according to this verse, this "unsealed" book will fully explain this connection, and the people will then learn that Jesus is the "Holy One of Israel." Therefore, any book that comes forth, claiming to be this "unsealed" book, will have to teach that Jesus is the "Holy One of Israel."

The fact that the "Holy One of Israel" is never mentioned, in the "New Testament," also provides proof that the "New Testament" is not this "unsealed" book.

Isaiah 29:20, "For the terrible one is brought to nought, and the scorner is consumed, and all that watch for iniquity are cut off:"

Interpretation: this "unsealed" book will have the power to put the **"terrible one"** (Satan) in his place. Therefore, this "unsealed" book will correct many of the false doctrines, and false theologies, taught in modern times. **"The scorner"** (those who deny the truthfulness of this book) will be **"consumed"** by fire, and those who **"watch for iniquity"** (those who ignore God's laws and commandments) will be completely **"cut off,"** from the presence of God. Therefore, this scripture is saying that this book will remove every excuse that the people will have, for not strictly obeying God's laws and commandments, to the best of their ability.

Isaiah 29:21, "That make a man an offender for a word, and lay a snare for him that reproveth in the gate, and turn aside the just for a thing of nought."

Interpretation: this verse explains that this "unsealed" book is a snare (or a trap), designed to capture those who refuse to believe, that this "unsealed" book contains the "words of God." These people will be considered an offender, against the "word of God," itself. When this verse says: **"turn aside the just for a thing of nought,"** this simply means that even though many people, including many ministers and priests, will scoff at this **"just"** book, they will have nothing to offer in its place. In other words, many ministers will proclaim that because we already have one bible in our possession, that we do not need another bible, or any more words from the hands of God. In their eyes, one book from God, is more than enough. What does this attitude reveal about the modern-day ministers and priests? What true Christian would ever say that we do not need to learn more about God and Jesus Christ? However, it seems that many ministers and priests, in the modern world, today, do not share our sentiment.

> **Isaiah 29:22, "Therefore thus saith the LORD, who redeemed Abraham, concerning the house of Jacob, Jacob shall not now be ashamed, neither shall his face now wax pale."**

Interpretation: this "unsealed" book, written for the "House of Ephraim," will restore the original blessings previously given to Jacob and Abraham. Before understanding, what this verse is talking about, it would be necessary to learn the following:

1. **Jacob had a dream that through his seed the families of the world would be blessed** (Genesis 28:12-15).
2. **The promises, given to Jacob, also included the earlier promises and blessings, given to Abraham** (Genesis 28:4).
3. **Jacob's name was changed to Israel** (Genesis 35:10).
4. **Joseph was the son of Jacob** (Israel) (Genesis 30: 22-25).
5. **Ephraim was the son of Joseph** (Genesis 41: 51-52).
6. **The original blessings and promises given to Jacob** (Israel), **and Abraham, were also given to Ephraim** (study Genesis 48).

Therefore, this verse is simply letting us know, that this "unsealed" book will fulfill the promises previously given to Jacob (Israel), Abraham, Joseph, and Ephraim.

> **Isaiah 29:23, "But when he seeth his children, the work of mine hands, in the midst of him, they shall sanctify my**

name, and sanctify the Holy One of Jacob, and shall fear the God of Israel."

Interpretation: Jacob's children (referring to the twelve tribes of Israel) will eventually receive this "unsealed" book in their hands. This is when they will sanctify and worship, Jesus Christ, and will recognize him as the Holy One of Jacob, and the "Holy one of Israel, and will fear (obey) the God of Israel. It needs to be understood that because the twelve tribes of Israel, were scattered around the world, means that this "unsealed" book will also spread, around the world. It should be mentioned that the "Book of Mormon" teaches about the "Holy One of Israel" about thirty-nine times.

Isaiah 29:24, "They also that erred in spirit shall come to understanding, and they that murmured shall learn doctrine."

Interpretation: this "unsealed" book will teach the people who once **"erred in spirit"** (misinterpreted the scriptures) so that they **"shall come to understanding,"** and **"those who murmured"** (those who could not understand the bible scriptures at all) **"shall learn doctrine."**

We learn from the prophecies of Isaiah, Ezekiel, and "John the Revelator" that another book (not the "Holy Bible") was scheduled to arrive on earth, through the hands of an angel. We were also informed that an uneducated man would receive this **"sealed"** book, in his hands, which he would then translate from its original unknown language (or lost language). This **"sealed"** book was scheduled to be **"unsealed,"** slightly before the boundaries for modern-day Lebanon are extended to the seacoast, in 1918. Notice that this "unsealed" book will also be seen with the "Holy Bible," and that both books will teach the gospel, as one book. This is because Ezekiel proclaimed that both books will become as **"one in thine hand."**

Earlier, when we discussed the prophecy of Amos, we discovered that the True Gospel of Jesus Christ disappeared, and was lost:

> "**Behold, the days come, saith the Lord God, that I will send a famine in the land, not a famine of bread, nor a thirst for water, but of hearing the words of the Lord: And they shall wander from sea to sea, and from the north even to the east, THEY SHALL RUN TO AND FRO TO SEEK THE WORD OF THE LORD, AND SHALL NOT FIND IT"** (Amos 8:11-12).

We also discovered that this was scheduled to happen, shortly after 70 A.D., after the temple in Jerusalem is destroyed. We then talked about another prophecy, provided by Daniel, which predicted that: **"many shall run to and fro and knowledge shall be increased:"**

> "**But thou, O Daniel, shut up the words, and seal the book, even to the time of the end: many shall run to and fro, and KNOWLEDGE SHALL BE INCREASED"** (Daniel 12:4).

When these two prophecies are combined, together, with the understanding that God will never change:

> "**For I am the Lord, I change not**" (Malachi 3:6).

> "**Jesus Christ the same yesterday, and today, and forever**" (Hebrews 13:8).

We begin to understand that God will use the same exact methods, during the last days, that he always used in the past. One method that God often used, during biblical times, was to command his chosen servants and prophets to write books. Some of these books were written to record the generations (Genesis 5:1). Moses was commanded to write a book, for a memorial, and to "rehearse it in the ears of Joshua" (Exodus 17:14). Moses wrote the "Book of the laws" (Deuteronomy 31:24-26). We also learn that Samuel wrote a book (1 Samuel 10:25). The "kings of Israel and Judah" wrote a book (1 Chronicles 9:1). Another book was written, referred to as: the "Book of the records of the Chronicles" (Esther 2:23; 6:1). Jeremiah also wrote a book (Jeremiah 36:2; 51:60). Ezekiel received a "book on a roll" to read and to study (Ezekiel 2:9-10; 3:1-4). The bible mentions the "Book of Life," which is a written record of the faithful believers, on earth (Exodus 32:33; Daniel 12:1; Phillip 4:3; Revelation 3:5; 13:8; 20:12; 21:27). A "book of remembrance" was also written (Malachi 3:16). As you can see, many different books were written, during biblical times, and when we study the "Book of Ecclesiastes," we learn: **"of making many books there is no end."**

"The words of the wise are as goads, and as nails fastened by the masters of assemblies, which are given from one shepherd. And Further, by these, my son, be admonished: OF MAKING MANY BOOKS THERE IS NO END; and much study is a weariness of the flesh" (Ecclesiastes 12:12).

Even though this scripture proves that many books were written, in the past, most modern-day ministers do not understand that another book was scheduled to arrive on earth, through the hands of an angel, during the "last days." The only book, which matches the bible prophecies that we just studied, is the "Book of Mormon." This book was published in 1830, which was slightly before the boundaries for modern-day Lebanon were extended, in 1918 (Isaiah 29:17). This book also teaches about the "Holy One of Israel" about 39 times.

Even though many of the ancient prophets kept a written record, of everything that they taught, many of their documents did not survive the test of time. Therefore, many of these documents were either lost, destroyed, or in some cases, were buried to keep them safe. Question: what do you think would happen, today, if some of these ancient manuscripts were suddenly discovered? Do you think that most modern-day ministers and priests would welcome, these ancient documents, with open arms? The fact remains that many of these ancient documents would immediately be rejected, by most modern-day ministers and priests, no matter what information that these documents contain. The simple fact that so many modern-day ministers reject, the "Book of Mormon," proves my point. It would not matter if some of the documents were written by Moses, or by Abraham, or by some other well-known prophet. Therefore, Christians should always remember how the bible scriptures, came into existence, in the first place. The bible is compilation of many ancient letters and manuscripts, previously written by the early prophets and disciples, which were later gathered up to create a book. As a result, if the prophets and disciples never kept any written records, we would not have the Holy Bible in our possession, today.

In fact, we learn from John that many things that Jesus did, were not even recorded:

"And there are also MANY OTHER THINGS which Jesus did, the which, if they should be written every one, I suppose that even the world itself could not contain the books that should be written. Amen" (John 21:25).

In modern times, Christians have been taught that the crucifixion and resurrection of Jesus, ended the ministry of Jesus, on earth. What most Christians have not been told, is the fact that Jesus can now do more today, then what he could ever have accomplished before his crucifixion. The fact that Jesus is a resurrected being, provides proof that Jesus can now travel around the world, without any physical limitations. Therefore, Christians need to understand that the ministry of Jesus did not end after his crucifixion, but it continued, and this is when he visited many different people, around the world. This is what Jesus was talking about in the following scripture:

> **"And other sheep I have, which are not of this fold: them also I must bring, and they shall hear my voice; and there shall be one fold, and one shepherd"** (John 10:16).

The fact that he visited other people, around the world, also means that many of these people kept a written record of the things, that Jesus taught. Therefore, the Holy Bible and the "Book of Mormon" are not the only books that we will ever receive, from the hands of God. Earlier, we discussed the following scriptures, which reveal that Jesus will remain in heaven **"until"** after the **"restitution of all things"** prophecy, is fulfilled:

> **"And he shall send Jesus Christ, which before was preached unto you: whom the heaven must receive UNTIL THE TIMES OF RESTITUTION OF ALL THINGS, which God hath spoken by the mouth of all his holy prophets since the world began"** (Acts 3:20-21).

During the time when the **"restitution of all things"** prophecy, will be fulfilled, is also when **"knowledge"** (about God and Jesus) **"shall be increased:"**

> **"But thou, O Daniel, shut up the words, and seal the book, even to the time of the end: many shall run to and fro, and knowledge shall be increased"** (Daniel 12:4).

This prophecy (Daniel 12:4) was not scheduled to be fulfilled, until after the "last days" arrived, during **"the time of the end."** The **"restitution of all things"** prophecy, raises several interesting questions, concerning the bible, itself. Why would the bible scriptures tell us about a **"restitution"** (or "restoration"), which would happen, sometime during the "last days," if the bible contains everything that we would ever need to know? What is missing from the bible scriptures, which is so important, that it would take a "restitution" (or "restoration") to "restore" this missing information on earth? Even though it was the fulfillment of this **"restitution of all things"** prophecy, during the "last days," which "restored" the "True Gospel of Jesus Christ" on earth, most modern days ministers have no idea that these "restoration" prophecies even exist.

When we combine the prophecies, concerning the "little book" (Revelation 10:8-10)," with the prophecies of Ezekiel and Isaiah, we learn that a "sealed" book was scheduled to arrive, on earth, through the hands of an angel? In accordance with Isaiah's prophecy (Isaiah 29:12), this "sealed" book was delivered to an uneducated man, who would then "unseal" this book. This uneducated man was none other than Prophet Joseph Smith, who only had a fourth-grade education, during that time. Here is the testimony of Prophet Joseph Smith, when he explains what happened, when he was visited by this angel:

> **"While I was thus in the act of calling upon God, I discovered a light appearing in my room, which continued to increase until the room was lighter than at noonday, when immediately a personage appeared at my bedside, standing in the air, for his feet did not touch the floor. He had on a loose robe of most exquisite whiteness. It was a whiteness beyond anything earthly I had ever seen; nor do I believe that any earthly thing could be made to appear so exceedingly white and brilliant. His hands were naked, and his arms also, a little above the wrist; so, also, were his feet naked, as were his legs, a little above the ankles. His head and neck were also bare. I could discover that he had**

no other clothing on but this robe, as it was open, so that I could see into his bosom. Not only was his robe exceedingly white, but his whole person was glorious beyond description, and his countenance truly like lightning. The room was exceedingly light, but not so very bright as immediately around his person. When I first looked upon him, I was afraid; but the fear soon left me. He called me by name, and said unto me that he was a messenger sent from the presence of God to me, and that his name was Moroni; that God had a work for me to do; and that my name should be had for good and evil among all nations, kindreds, and tongues, or that it should be both good and evil spoken of among all people. He said there was a book deposited, written upon gold plates, giving an account of the former inhabitants of this continent, and the source from whence they sprang. He also said that the fullness of the everlasting Gospel was contained in it, as delivered by the Savior to the ancient inhabitants; Also, that there were two stones in silver bows—and these stones, fastened to a breastplate, constituted what is called the Urim and Thummim—deposited with the plates; and the possession and use of these stones were what constituted "seers" in ancient or former times; and that God had prepared them for the purpose of translating the book" (Joseph Smith History 1:30-35).

"The Church of Jesus Christ of Latter-day Saints" is the only church, on earth, which fulfilled the bible prophecies that we just discussed. This church fulfilled Daniel's "ten kings" prophecy, when it was established on earth, between the years of 1806 and 1848, during the reign of the "ten kings." In fact, this church was officially established on earth in 1830, slightly before the fifth kingdom was removed from power, by the French Revolution (July,1830). Prophet Joseph Smith fulfilled Daniel's "sanctuary be cleansed" prophecy (Daniel 8:13-14), when he was martyred in Carthage, Illinois, on June 27, 1844.

In the following scriptures, we are told about the attitude that many modern-day Christians will display, toward the "Book of Mormon," when they first hear about this book.

> "But behold, there shall be many—at that day when I shall proceed to do a marvelous work among them, that I may remember my covenants which I have made unto the children of men, that I may set my hand again the second time to recover my people, which are of the house of Israel; And also, that I may remember the promises which I have made unto thee, Nephi, and also unto thy father, that I would remember your seed; and that the words of your seed should proceed forth out of my mouth unto your seed; and my words shall hiss forth unto the ends of the earth, for a standard unto my people, which are of the house of Israel; And because my words shall hiss forth—many of the Gentiles shall say: A Bible! A Bible! We have got a Bible, and there cannot be any more Bible. But thus saith the Lord God: O fools, they shall have a Bible; and it shall proceed forth from the Jews, mine ancient covenant people. And what thank they the Jews for the Bible which they receive from them? Yea, what do the Gentiles mean? Do they remember the travails, and the labors, and the pains of the Jews, and their diligence unto me, in bringing forth salvation unto the Gentiles?"

> "O ye Gentiles, have ye remembered the Jews, mine ancient covenant people? Nay; but ye have cursed them, and have hated them, and have not sought to recover them. But behold, I will return all these things upon your own heads;

for I the Lord have not forgotten my people. Thou fool, that shall say: A Bible, we have got a Bible, and we need no more Bible. Have ye obtained a Bible save it were by the Jews? Know ye not that there are more nations than one? Know ye not that I, the Lord your God, have created all men, and that I remember those who are upon the isles of the sea; and that I rule in the heavens above and in the earth beneath; and I bring forth my word unto the children of men, yea, even upon all the nations of the earth? Wherefore murmur ye, because that ye shall receive more of my word? Know ye not that the testimony of two nations is a witness unto you that I am God, that I remember one nation like unto another? Wherefore, I speak the same words unto one nation like unto another. And when the two nations shall run together the testimony of the two nations shall run together also. And I do this that I may prove unto many that I am the same yesterday, today, and forever; and that I speak forth my words according to mine own pleasure. And because that I have spoken one word ye need not suppose that I cannot speak another; for my work is not yet finished; neither shall it be until the end of man, neither from that time henceforth and forever."

"Wherefore, because that ye have a Bible ye need not suppose that it contains all my words; neither need ye suppose that I have not caused more to be written. For I command all men, both in the east and in the west, and in the north, and in the south, and in the islands of the sea, that they shall write the words which I speak unto them; for out of the books which shall be written I will judge the world, every man according to their works, according to that which is written.

For behold, I shall speak unto the Jews and they shall write it; and I shall also speak unto the Nephites and they shall write it; and I shall also speak unto the other tribes of the house of Israel, which I have led away, and they shall write it; and I shall also speak unto all nations of the earth and they shall write it. And it shall come to pass that the Jews shall have the words of the Nephites, and the Nephites shall have the words of the Jews; and the Nephites and the Jews shall have the words of the lost tribes of Israel; and the lost tribes of Israel shall have the words of the Nephites and the Jews. And it shall come to pass that my people, which are of the house of Israel, shall be gathered home unto the lands of their possessions; and my word also shall be gathered in one. And I will show unto them that fight against my word and against my people, who are of the house of Israel, that I am God, and that I covenanted with Abraham that I would remember his seed forever" (2 Nephi 29:1-14).

The "Book of Mormon" also teaches, how to recognize the difference, between good and evil:

"Wherefore, a man being evil cannot do that which is good; neither will he give a good gift." For behold, a bitter fountain cannot bring forth good water; neither can a good fountain bring forth bitter water; wherefore, a man being a servant of the devil cannot follow Christ; and if he follow Christ he cannot be a servant of the devil. Wherefore, all things which are good cometh of God; and that which is evil cometh of the devil; for the devil is an enemy unto God, and fighteth against him continually, and inviteth and enticeth to sin, and to do that which is evil continually. But behold, that which is of God inviteth and enticeth to do good continually; wherefore, everything which inviteth and

enticeth to do good, and to love God, and to serve him, is inspired of God. Wherefore, take heed, my beloved brethren, that ye do not judge that which is evil to be of God, or that which is good and of God to be of the devil. For behold, my brethren, it is given unto you to judge, that ye may know good from evil; and the way to judge is as plain, that ye may know with a perfect knowledge, as the daylight is from the dark night. For behold, the Spirit of Christ is given to every man, that he may know good from evil; wherefore, I show unto you the way to judge; for everything which inviteth to do good, and to persuade to believe in Christ, is sent forth by the power and gift of Christ; wherefore ye may know with a perfect knowledge it is of God (Moroni 7:10-16).

In either case, it was "The Church of Jesus Christ of Latter-day Saints," which fulfilled the bible prophecies that we discussed. It should also be remembered that this church also fulfilled the following prophecy:

"And it shall come to pass in the last days, that the mountain of the Lord's house shall be established in the top of the mountains, and shall be exalted above the hills; and all nations shall flow unto it" (Isaiah 2:2).

"But in the last days it shall come to pass, that the mountain of the house of the Lord shall be established in the top of the mountains, and it shall be exalted above the hills; and people shall flow unto it" (Micha 4:1).

The fact that the headquarters for this church is located, in the top of the Rocky Mountains, proves that this church is fulfilling the prophecies of Isaiah, and Micha (Isaiah 2:2; Micah 4:1). This is one more prophecy, which proves that "The Church of Jesus Christ of Latter-day Saints," is the official "Kingdom of God" on earth, today.

If you still have some doubt, concerning "The Church of Jesus Christ of Latter-day Saints," then simply obey the following instructions:

> **"And when ye shall receive these things, I would exhort you that ye would ask God, the Eternal Father, in the name of Christ, if these things are not true; and if ye shall ask with a sincere heart, with real intent, having faith in Christ, he will manifest the truth of it unto you, by the power of the Holy Ghost. And by the power of the Holy Ghost ye may know the truth of all things"** (Moroni 10:4-5).

"Book of Daniel"
Chapter 11 King James Version

There are many ministers who teach their congregations, that the prophecies in this chapter, are prophecies for the future. What these ministers have failed to understand, is the fact that the events in this chapter began in 538 B.C., after "Cyrus the Great" ("Darius the Mede") attacked Babylon, and ends in 96 A.D., after the death of Caesar Domitian. Even though these prophecies were fulfilled, many centuries before we were born, they are still very interesting to study. In fact, these prophecies prove that God knows all things, before they happen, and that Daniel was a true Prophet of God. It should also be noted that from this point forward, many of the prophecies that will be discussed, were previously discussed in several other prophecies. To avoid confusion, when discussing these new prophecies, this repetition was necessary to make these new prophecies understandable.

> **Daniel 11:1, "Also I in the first year of Darius the Mede, even I stood to confirm and to strengthen him."**

Interpretation: the first year that "Cyrus the Great" ("Darius the Mede") ruled, over Babylon, was 538 B.C. It needs to be understood that Daniel would not have made the statement: **"even I stood to**

confirm and to strengthen him," if "Darius the Mede" was his enemy. Daniel recognized that this person was King Cyrus, who received the title as the "King of the Medes," when he succeeded his father, in 559 B.C.

> **Daniel 11:2, "And now will I shew thee the truth, Behold, there shall stand up yet three kings in Persia: and the fourth shall be far richer than they all: and by his strength through his riches he shall stir up all against the realm of Grecia."**

Interpretation: from this prophecy, we learn that: **"there shall stand up yet three kings in Persia,"** after the reign of King Cyrus ("Darius the Mede") is over. This prophecy is talking about the three kings, who would receive the "Darius" title, after the reign of King Cyrus ("Darius 0") comes to an end: "Darius I;" "Darius II;" and "Darius III." Notice that the fourth king, Darius III, was also predicted to go to war against the Macedonian-Greek Empire: **"the realm of Grecia."** "Darius III" fulfilled this prophecy, when he went to war against "Alexander the Great," who was the ruler of the Macedonian-Greek Empire.

Note: in the next set of prophecies, from verses three through nineteen, we learn about the Macedonian-Greek Empire, and how this empire was created.

> **Daniel 11:3, "And a mighty king shall stand up, that shall rule with great dominion, and do according to his will."**

> **Daniel 11:4, "And when he shall stand up, his kingdom shall be broken, and shall be divided toward the four winds of heaven; and not to his posterity, nor according to his dominion which he ruled: for his kingdom shall be plucked up, even for others beside those."**

Interpretation: these two verses are talking about the entire history of the Macedonian-Greek Empire. Therefore, when this prophecy says: **"And when he shall stand up, his kingdom shall be broken,"** this is talking about the condition of Macedonia, when Philip II took control. In a very short time, Phillip II expanded this territory to include the Paionians, the Thracians, the Illyrians, and the territories of Monastir and Gevgelija. In other words, it was Phillip II who created the "Macedonian-Greek Empire." When this prophecy says: **"and shall be divided toward the four winds of heaven,"** this is talking about what happened, after the death of "Alexander the Great." This is when the "Macedonian-Greek Empire" was divided up, which eventually evolved into four powerful dynasties: the Antigonid dynasty; the Ptolemaic dynasty; the Seleucid dynasty; and the Attalid dynasty. Notice that this prophecy also predicted that the "Macedonian-Greek Empire," would not remain in the hands of any descendants, of Phillip II. Meaning of: **"and not to his posterity."** The prophecy which reads: **"nor according to his dominion which he ruled,"** also means that after the death of "Alexander the Great," the "Macedonian-Greek Empire" would never be united under one powerful leader, again. When the prophecy says: **"for his kingdom shall be plucked up,"** this was predicting that this kingdom would eventually be defeated in battle, just like the other kingdoms that existed before it: **"even for others beside those."** In other words, the Macedonian-Greek Empire would eventually be defeated in battle, just like the Babylonian and Persian Empires.

> **Daniel 11:5, "And the king of the south shall be strong, and one of his princes; and he shall be strong above him, and have dominion; his dominion shall be a great dominion."**

Interpretation: this prophecy is talking about "King Alexander of Epirus," as the **"king of the south,"** which predicts that his son Pyrrhus, who was a prince over one of the Alexandrian states, would eventually rule over a greater kingdom than his father's. Meaning of: **"he shall** be strong above him, and have dominion; his dominion shall be a great dominion." Pyrrhus, the son of "King Alexander of Epirus," fulfilled this prophecy, because he eventually ruled over a much greater kingdom than his father.

> **Daniel 11:6, "And in the end of years they shall join themselves together; for the king's daughter of the south shall come to the king of the north to make an agreement: but she shall not retain the power of the arm; neither shall he stand, nor his arm: but she shall be given up, and they that brought her, and he that begat her, and he that strengthened her in these times."**

Interpretation: this prophecy is talking about the marriage agreement, which was made between King Philip II and the King of Epirus: **"for the king's daughter of the south shall come to the king of the north to make an agreement."** The prophecy, which says: **"but she shall not retain the power of the arm,"** is talking about Olympias, and her **"arm"** in marriage to Phillip II. Olympias, was the daughter of the "King of Epirus" (the "king of the south"), who married Philip II (the "king of the north"), and eventually had a son by the name of Alexander ("Alexander the Great"). This prophecy is predicting that Olympias would someday take control of Macedonia, after Phillip II is assassinated, and after "Alexander the Great" dies. This prophecy then predicts that her marriage to Phillip II, **"the power of the arm,"** would not help her keep control of her kingdom. Nor would the power of her father: **"he that begat her;"** nor would the power of her son, "Alexander the Great:" **"he that strengthened her in these times."** The prophecy: **"neither shall he stand,"** is talking about the fact that her husband, Philip II, would be assassinated. The prophecy: **"nor his arm,"** is referring to the fact that even though Olympias was the wife of Phillip II, this would not help her keep control of Macedonia. In other words, Olympias would be completely alone, in her kingdom, after the death of her father, her husband, and her son. As a result, she would not receive any help from the Macedonians, to help her keep control of Macedonia: **"she shall be given up."** She was eventually defeated, and killed, by Cassander (one of Alexander's generals).

Daniel 11:7, "But out of the branch of her roots shall one stand up in his estate, which shall come with an army, and shall enter into the fortress of the king of the north, and shall deal against them, and shall prevail:"

Interpretation: **"But out of the branch of her roots,"** is now talking about the son of Olympias: "Alexander the Great." The **"king of the north,"** in this verse, is talking about the different kings who ruled in Thrace. It needs to be understood that the prophecies, concerning the kings of the north and the south, often change, because of geography. Therefore, the "king of the north" would become the "king of the south," as soon as another northern king arrives on the scene. In this case, "Alexander the Great" is now the king of the south, because the king of the north is referring to the kings of the Illyrians, and the Triballi tribes in the territory of Thrace, which was located north of Macedonia. Notice that Alexander was predicted to defeat these kings: **"shall deal against them, and shall prevail."**

Daniel 11:8, "And shall also carry captives into Egypt their gods, with their princes, and with their precious vessels of silver and of gold; and he shall continue more years than the king of the north."

Interpretation: from this prophecy we learn that "Alexander the Great" was not only predicted to conquer Egypt, but that he would also introduce the Greek gods, to the Egyptians. Many Macedonians thought that when Alexander took the Greek gods, with him, that this is when the Greek gods became his captives. He successfully captured several princes with their **"precious vessels of silver and of gold."** The prophecy: **"and he shall continue more years than the king of the north,"** is referring to "Darius III," who became the ruler over the northern province of the Persian Empire. It is a historical fact that "Alexander the Great" did live longer than "Darius III" (the "king of the north"), because "Darius III" was killed in 330 B.C., while Alexander lived seven years longer, and died in 323 B.C. This same prophecy: **"and he shall continue more years than the king of the north,"** could also be applied to "Artaxerxes V," who succeeded "Darius III," because he was captured and killed by "Alexander the Great."

Note: after the death of "Alexander the Great," the "Macedonian-Greek Empire" ceased to exist, as a unified kingdom, under the rule of one powerful military leader. In the following prophecies, from verses nine through nineteen, we learn what happened after the death of Alexander. This is when the kingdom was divided up among his powerful generals.

Daniel 11:9, "So the king of the south shall come into his kingdom, and shall return into his own land."

Interpretation: in 320 B.C., after the death of Alexander, a powerful general by the name of Antipater (the new king of the south) returned to Macedonia from Greece, to claim his rightful place as the Supreme Regent over the Macedonian-Greek Empire. Shortly thereafter, he died from an illness, which somehow resulted in Polyperchon being appointed as the next regent over this Empire, and not the legitimate heir Cassander, who was the son of Antipater. This appointment soon caused a war between Polyperchon and Cassander.

Daniel 11:10, "But his sons shall be stirred up, and shall assemble a multitude of great forces: and one shall certainly come, and overflow, and pass through: then shall he return, and be stirred up, even to his fortress."

Interpretation: after Polyperchon was appointed as the new regent, Cassander the son of Antipater, and Alexander the son of "Alexander the Great," joined forces and created a powerful army to fight against Polyperchon: **"But his sons shall be stirred up, and shall assemble a multitude of great forces."** This prophecy predicts that Cassander would successfully defeat Polyperchon in battle: **"and one shall certainly come, and overflow, and pass through."** After Cassander returned to Macedonia, he soon realized that another war was looming, sometime in the near future: **"then shall he return, and be stirred up, even to his fortress."** It needs to be noted that Alexander, the son of "Alexander the Great," was killed in the battle against Polyperchon, which helps explain why the Macedonian Empire would not be passed down to any descendants of Phillip II, which began to fulfill the prophecy in verse four: **"and not to his posterity."**

> **Daniel 11:11, "And the king of the south shall be moved with choler, and shall come forth and fight with him, even the king of the north: and he shall set forth a great multitude; but the multitude shall be given into his hand."**

Interpretation: when Cassander (**"the king of the south"**) created his great army, it also included "Antigonus of Asia Minor" (**"king of the north"**), who was a very powerful military leader. Even though Polyperchon also had a powerful army of his own (**"a great multitude"**), to fight against Cassander, he was soon defeated: **"but the multitude shall be given into his hand."**

> **Daniel 11:12, "And when he hath taken away the multitude, his heart shall be lifted up; and he shall cast down many ten thousands: but he shall not be strengthened by it."**

Interpretation: sometime after the battle with Polyperchon was over, Cassander then decided to attack Olympias, the mother of "Alexander the Great." As a result, Olympias was killed, and shortly thereafter, Alexander's widow and her newborn son were also killed. Once again, it was the death of Alexander's newborn son, which guaranteed that the Macedonian Empire would never be passed down to any descendants of Phillip II: **"and not to his posterity."** Even though Cassander successfully conquered the Macedonian territory, during that time, it did not remain in his hands for very long: **"but he shall not be strengthened by it."**

Daniel 11:13, "For the king of the north shall return, and shall set forth a multitude greater than the former, and shall certainly come after certain years with a great army and with much riches."

Interpretation: Cassander recognized that "Antigonus I" (**"king of the north"**) was a very dangerous adversary, who could easily become a serious threat, if he decided to use his substantial wealth to build a great army. From this prophecy we learn that this was predicted to happen, when **"the king of the north shall return"** with a great army, which is much greater than what he had before: **"and shall set forth a multitude greater than the former."** A few years, after Polyperchon was defeated in battle, "Antigonus I" made plans to attack Macedonia: **"and shall certainly come after certain years with a great army."**

Daniel 11:14, "And in those times there shall be many stand up against the king of the south: also the robbers of thy people shall exalt themselves to establish the vision; but they shall fall."

Interpretation: soon after "Antigonus I" became the king over Macedonia (the king of the south), he was killed in battle, which created a vacuum of leadership. It needs to be understood that the Macedonians shared one common dream, or vision, during that time. The people of Macedonia hoped and dreamed, that someday Macedonia would once again become a great and powerful kingdom, ruled by one strong and powerful military leader, like they experienced under the rule of "Alexander the Great." After "Antigonus I" was killed, this created a vacuum, which caused many different groups to fight for control over Macedonia. These different groups (and gangs) were hoping to fulfill this Macedonian dream, or vision: **"the robbers of thy people shall exalt themselves to establish the vision."** Of course, the historical record proves that these attempts failed: **"but they shall fall."**

> **Daniel 11:15, "So the king of the north shall come, and cast up a mount, and take the most fenced cities: and the arms of the south shall not withstand, neither his chosen people, neither shall there be and strength to withstand."**

Interpretation: as predicted in verse thirteen, the king of the north ("Antigonus I") did attack, and he did **"cast up a mount,"** and he did conquer the **"fenced cities."** When this verse says: **"the arms of the south shall not withstand, neither his chosen people,"** this was predicting that Antigonus I" (the king of the north) would successfully conquer Macedonia and its powerful military army. And when this verse says: **"neither shall there be and strength to withstand,"** simply meant that "Antigonus I" would not be able to finish what he started (**"to withstand"**), because he would die in battle. This is when "Demetrius I," the son of "Antigonus I," arrived on the scene.

> **Daniel 11:16, "But he that cometh against him shall do according to his own will, and none shall stand before him: and he shall stand in the glorious land, which by his hand shall be consumed."**

Interpretation: this prophecy: **"But he that cometh against him,"** is referring to "Demetrius I," as the individual who would continue to fight against Cassander, and **"shall do according to his own will, and none shall stand before him."** Militarily speaking, "Demetrius I" did **"according to his own will,"** and no one had the military strength to stop him: **"none shall stand before him."** "Demetrius I" also fulfilled the prophecy, concerning **"the glorious land,"** after he conquered Athens. Even in modern times, the city of Athens is still referred to as **"the glorious land,"** because of its beautiful ancient temples. This scripture is often misinterpreted, in modern times, because many bible scholars have erroneously assumed that the phrase: **"the glorious land,"** is talking about the land of Israel, and Judah. As a result, this has caused many scholars to also misinterpret, the following scripture:

Daniel 11:17, "He shall also set his face to enter with the strength of his whole kingdom, and upright ones with him; thus shall he do: and he shall give him the daughter of women, corrupting her: but she shall not stand on his side, neither be for him."

Interpretation: this prophecy is still talking about "Demetrius I," who became the king over Macedonia, and continued to fight against Cassander, and many others: **"set his face to enter with the strength of his whole kingdom."** He established the concept of personal freedom: **"and upright ones with him."** During his battles, he successfully freed the city of Athens, from the hands of Cassander: **"thus shall he do."** As a result, the people of Athens invited "Demetrius I" to stay in the Parthenon, where they worshipped their virgin god, Minerva. Sometime later, after the Athenians began to worship "Demetrius I" as a minor god (a tutelary), someone suggested that "Demetrius I" should marry Minerva, their virgin god: **"and he shall give him the daughter of women, corrupting her."** Because this wedding was never performed, and because Minerva did not really exist as a living person, explains why the prophecy: **"but she shall not stand on his side, neither be for him"** was fulfilled. If this marriage was performed, Minerva would have lost her official standing as "a virgin god," from that time forward, which would have corrupted her forever: **"corrupting her."** It would have been a very serious error which could never be corrected.

Daniel 11:18, "After this shall he turn his face unto the isles, and shall take many: but a prince for his own behalf shall cause the reproach offered by him to cease; without his own reproach he shall cause it to turn upon him."

Daniel 11:19, "Then he shall turn his face toward the fort of his own land: but he shall stumble and fall, and not be found."

Interpretation: after "Demetrius I," freed Athens, he then turned his attention toward the islands: **"After this shall he turn his face unto the isles, and shall take many."** This is when he successfully captured Cypress. "Demetrius I" later returned to Athens, again, but this time the Athenian people turned against him and forced him to leave. "Demetrius I" would later return to Athens again, to free the Athenians from another tyrant, by the name of Lachares. This is when "Demetrius I" forgave the Athenian people for their **"reproach"** against him, which fulfilled the prophecy **"but a prince for his own behalf shall cause the reproach offered by him to cease."** When he returned to Macedonia, he was surprised that the political and military situation between Pyrrhus, Ptolemy, and Lysimachus had changed. After "Demetrius I" fought a few battles, against them, he was forced to leave Macedonia. In other words, because Demetrius neglected the Macedonian people, for such a long time, the people turned against him: **"without his own reproach he shall cause it to turn upon him."** He then made another serious error when he decided to attack Syria. This is when he was captured and eventually died in prison in 283 B.C. It was this serious mistake, which fulfilled the prophecy **"but he shall stumble and fall, and not be found."**

His son tried his best, to get him released from prison, but failed. However, after his death his body was eventually returned to his son, for burial.

Note: verses 20 through 22, talk about the Hellenistic Seleucid period, of the Greek Empire.

> **Daniel 11:20, "Then shall stand up in his estate a raiser of taxes in the glory of the kingdom: but within few days he shall be destroyed, neither in anger, nor in battle."**

Interpretation: this prophecy was fulfilled approximately one hundred years after the death of "Demetrius I." During the reign of Seleucus IV Philopater, he set out to raise taxes, to pay for the incredible debt that was incurred, during the war years. He soon decided to confiscate the money from the Jewish temple. On the return trip home, he was assassinated by Heliodorus, who fulfilled the prophecy: **"but within few days he shall be destroyed, neither in anger, nor in battle."** This prophecy was fulfilled in 176 B.C.

> **Daniel 11:21, "And in his estate shall stand up a vile person, to whom they shall NOT GIVE the honour of the kingdom: but he shall come in peaceably, and obtain the kingdom by flatteries."**

Interpretation: many scholars have assumed that this verse is talking about Antiochus IV Epiphanes. Even though I agree that he was a very **"vile person,"** he received **"the honour of the kingdom"** when he became the coregent, over the Seleucid Empire, between the years of 175 and 164 B.C. Therefore, because he received **"the honour of the kingdom,"** provides proof that he was not the person who fulfilled this prophecy: **"to whom they shall NOT GIVE the honour of the kingdom."** However, there was another **"vile person,"** who **did** not receive **"the honour of the kingdom,"** and this person was his brother "Demetrius I Soter." He was a very **"vile person,"** because "Demetrius I Soter" murdered his 11-year old nephew (Antiochus V Eupator), who was the legitimate heir to the throne, in hopes of gaining control over this empire. The fact that the Roman Senate **never gave** the **"honour of the kingdom,"** to "Demetrius I Soter," confirms that he was the **"vile person"** in this prophecy. When this prophecy says: **"but he shall come in peaceably, and obtain the kingdom by flatteries,"** this is now talking about a different individual, who falsely claimed that he was the legitimate heir to the throne. The fact that so many bible scholars assumed that "Antiochus IV Epiphanes," fulfilled the first part of this prophecy, is why they often fail to solve the second half of this prophecy. The second half was fulfilled, by Alexander Balas, who falsely claimed that he was the legitimate son of Antiochus IV Epiphanes. Therefore, because this claim was false, and because the Roman Senate supported this false claim against "Demetrius I Soter," provides proof that Alexander Balas obtained his **"kingdom by flatteries."** In other words, he convinced the Roman Senate to support his false claim, against "Demetrius I Soter." As a result, Balas was appointed as the new king, over Syria.

Daniel 11:22, "And with the arms of a flood shall they be overflown from before him, and shall be broken; yea, also the prince of the covenant."

Interpretation: this prophecy: **"with the arms of a flood"** was fulfilled in 145 B.C., when a **"flood"** of soldiers defeated Alexander Balas, during the "Battle of Antioch." Sometime later he was assassinated by a Nabataean prince: **"and shall be broken."** Because this prince was an ally of the Roman Empire, this prophecy also predicted that sometime in the distant future, this same empire (the Roman Empire) would kill the **"prince of the covenant."** The **"prince of the covenant"** is referring to Jesus. In other words, because Balas was killed by someone in the Roman Empire: **"and shall be broken,"** meant that sometime in the future, the Roman Empire would **"also"** kill **"the prince of the covenant"** (Jesus).

Note: verses 23 through 45, talk about the Roman Empire, between the years of 60 B.C to 96 A.D. This time period is often referred to as: "the reign of the twelve Caesars." It was during this time period, when Jesus was born; when Jesus began his ministry; when Jesus was crucified; and when Jerusalem, and the temple were destroyed. It should be noted that Daniel talks about the Roman Empire, many times in his prophecies, which also explains the important role that this kingdom was scheduled to play, during the "last days."

> **Daniel 11:23, "and after the league made with him he shall work deceitfully: for he shall come up, and shall become strong with a small people."**

Interpretation: this verse is now talking about Julius Caesar, who received his power from the Roman Senate: **"he became strong with a small people."** The **"league,"** is referring to the "first triumvirate," which was a political alliance that Julius Caesar made in 60 B.C., with two other men: March Anthony (Marcus Linius Crassus) and Pompey (Gnaeus Pompeius Magnus).

> **Daniel 11:24, "He shall enter peaceably even upon the fattest places of the province; and he shall do that which his fathers have not done, nor his fathers' fathers; he shall scatter among them the prey, and spoil, and riches: yea, and he shall forecast his devices against the strong holds, even for a time."**

Interpretation: after Julius Caesar was assassinated, Octavian became the next Roman Emperor, who soon accepted the religious title of

Augustus (meaning: the exalted one). When he accepted the religious title of "Augustus," this was something that his father Julius Caesar never did, nor any of the other Roman Caesars, who preceded him: **"and he shall do that which his fathers have not done, nor his fathers' fathers."** Augustus (Octavian) established the right of the Roman soldiers to share in the spoils, and the riches of war: **"he shall scatter among them the prey, and spoil, and riches."** The Roman military would often use ingenious military devices, and machines, against their enemies: **"and he shall forecast his devices against the strong holds."**

Daniel 11:25, "And he shall stir up his power and his courage against the king of the south with a great army; and the king of the south shall be stirred up to battle with a very great and mighty army; "but he shall not stand: for they shall forecast devices against him."

Daniel 11:26, "Yea, they that feed of the portion of his meat shall destroy him, and his army shall overflow: and many shall fall down slain."

Daniel 11:27, "And both these kings' hearts shall be to do mischief, and they shall speak lies at one table; but it shall not prosper: for yet the end shall be at the time appointed."

Interpretation: these three verses are now explaining the stormy relationship, which existed between Augustus Caesar, and Marc Anthony. The treaty of Brundisium, established that Augustus Caesar would control the western part of the empire; Marc Anthony the east; and Lipidus the continent of Africa. We learn from this prophecy that Augustus (the king of the north), and Marc Anthony (the king of the south), would eventually go to battle. This is when the king of the south (Marc Anthony) would be defeated: **"but he shall not stand: for they shall forecast devices against him."** Because Marc Anthony was a very powerful military leader, in the Roman Empire, also meant that he received a lot of his military supplies from the hands of Augustus Caesar, which explains why this prophecy proclaims: **"they that feed of the portion of his meat shall destroy him."** In other words, Marc Anthony was predicted to be defeated by the same individual, who provided him with his military supplies. It was during the treaty of Brundisium, when both men lied at this table, and did not reveal their true motives: **"And both these kings' hearts shall be to do mischief, and they shall speak lies at one table."** They later met in battle, to settle their disagreements, and this is when Augustus Caesar defeated Marc Anthony. After his defeat, Marc Anthony committed suicide, and this fulfilled the prophecy: **"for yet the end shall be at the time appointed."** Marc Anthony died in 30 B.C.

> **Daniel 11:28, "Then shall he return into his land with great riches; and his heart shall be against the holy covenant; and he shall do exploits, and return to his own land."**

Interpretation: after the war with Marc Anthony was over, Augustus Caesar (Octavian) returned to Rome: **"Then shall he return into his land with great riches."** Sometime in 6 A.D., he then decided that Rome should appoint the High Priests, in Jerusalem: **"his heart shall be against the holy covenant."** This decision caused a Jewish revolt which was soon brought under control. Augustus would often return to Rome after his military conquests: **"and he shall do exploits, and return to his own land."**

Note: in the following prophecies, the people in Judah, Israel, and Jerusalem are being warned that they will eventually be conquered, by the Roman Empire.

> **Daniel 11:29, At the time appointed he shall return, and come toward the south; but it shall not be as the former, or as the latter.**

"At the time appointed" is referring to the earlier prophecies, which predicted exactly when the temple, in Jerusalem, would be destroyed. This prophecy is talking about the First Roman Jewish War, and what was scheduled to happen, during that time. A Jewish rebellion began shortly after the Romans plundered the temple in Jerusalem. As a result, the Roman military strongholds were overrun, which forced the Roman Soldiers to flee Jerusalem. The Romans then responded to this rebellion, by sending in the Syrian Army, under the leadership of a Roman General, by the name of Cestius Gallus. It was during the "Battle of Beth Horon," when this army was ambushed, and over 6,000 Roman soldiers were slaughtered. The **"former,"** in this prophecy, is referring to what happened after the Romans plundered the temple, which forced the Roman military to leave Jerusalem: this was the Romans first response. The **"latter,"** in this prophecy, is talking about the second Roman response, when the Syrian army was sent to end this rebellion. This great military loss caused the Romans to rethink their position, and this is when they decided to respond to this Jewish rebellion, with a much larger military force. This last and final response was predicted to be quite different, from the first response (the **"former"**), when the Romans were forced to leave Jerusalem. This last and final response would also be quite different from the last response (the **"latter"**) when the Syrian soldiers were slaughtered. Therefore, the Romans decided that they would not make the same mistakes again. They would not be forced to leave Jerusalem, like the **"former"** encounter, and they would not be defeated in battle, like the **"latter"** encounter.

> **Daniel 11:30, "For the ships of Chittim shall come against him: therefore he shall be grieved, and return, and have indignation against the holy covenant: so shall he do; he shall even return, and have intelligence with them that forsake the holy covenant."**

Interpretation: this prophecy is talking about the events, which would lead to the destruction of Jerusalem, Judah, and Israel. Because the Roman army often travelled in ships, this prophecy is explaining how the Roman troops would arrive on the shores in Judah, and Israel: **"For the ships of Chittim shall come against him."** The word "Chittim" is possibly referring to some ancient seaport, in Cyprus, or another seaport that the Romans would often use, to transport their soldiers to battle. The fact that Cypress was a Roman province, during that time, also meant that Cypress had to provide some military support to the Romans: this support came in the form of supplying the Roman army, with the necessary ships, to carry out their military battles. Understand; the local Roman garrisons in Jerusalem, tried to control the Jewish revolt when it first began, but were forced to leave. The Romans then sent the Syrian military, under the leadership of Cestius Gallus, which was also a complete failure. The Romans third response was predicted to be quite different, because this final response would result in the complete destruction of Israel, Judah, and Jerusalem. This last response was quite different, because the Romans were determined to settle this issue, once and for all. Nero was the adopted son of Caesar Claudius, and after his death, Nero immediately returned to Rome: **"therefore he shall be grieved, and return."**

As a result, Nero assigned his son, General Vespasian to take charge of this Roman-Jewish war. General Vespasian, and his son Titus, attacked Judah with a large military force, which eventually resulted in the complete destruction of Jerusalem and the temple. To fully understand, this prophecy, requires that we also understand the meaning behind the words: **"holy covenant."** Nero despised the Christians and killed them in great numbers. Through the process of murdering these innocent Christians, Nero had openly displayed to the entire world his contempt and disgust for the **"holy covenant"** of God, which included the commandment: "Thou shalt not kill." The prophecy: **"he shall even return, and have intelligence with them that forsake the holy** covenant," is referring to the military forces that Nero sent to destroy Israel, and Jerusalem. This time the military was fully prepared, **"and have intelligence with them,"** to win this war. Understand; because the Jewish people turned their backs on Jesus, also meant that they turned their backs on the holy covenant: **"forsake the holy covenant."** As a result, the Jewish people received a great punishment, and this is when Jerusalem and the temple were destroyed, by the Roman army.

> **Daniel 11:31, "And arms shall stand on his part, and they shall pollute the sanctuary of strength, and shall take away the daily sacrifice, and shall place the abomination that maketh desolate."**

Interpretation: this prophecy is now explaining what happened during the reign of the Roman Empire, and the important role that it played, in the destruction of Israel, Judah, Jerusalem, the temple, and the crucifixion of Jesus. When this verse says: **"And arms shall stand on his part,"** this is referring to the powerful Roman military, under the rule of the Caesar. When it says: **"and they shall pollute the sanctuary of strength,"** this is talking about what happened when the Roman army plundered and destroyed the temple, in Jerusalem. It was also the Roman Empire that crucified Jesus: **"and shall take away the daily sacrifice."** The prophecy: **"and shall place the abomination that maketh desolate"** began to be fulfilled, shortly after Israel, Judah, and the temple in Jerusalem were destroyed. This is when **"the abomination that maketh desolate"** (the apostasy), which was previously predicted by Amos (Amos 8), began to spread around the world.

In the next set of prophecies, we learn about the spiritual damage, that the temple destruction inflicted on the entire world.

> **Daniel 11:32, "And such as do wickedly against the covenant shall be corrupt by flatteries: but the people that do know their God shall be strong, and do exploits."**

Interpretation: this prophecy is talking about the true gospel, and how this gospel became corrupted, when the ministers began to use **"flatteries,"** to build up their individual ministries: **"the covenant shall be corrupt by flatteries."** However, there were some faithful Christians who remained strong, in their faith, and continued to teach the True Gospel of Jesus Christ to others: **"but the people that do know their God shall be strong, and do exploits."** In other words, we learn from this prophecy that two different gospels existed, during that time. One gospel was corrupted by the false ministers, because they used **"flatteries,"** to build up their individual ministries. The other gospel, which was not corrupted, was taught by the early and faithful Christians, who knew their God. Therefore, one gospel was true, while the other gospel was false.

Daniel 11:33, "And they that understand among the people shall instruct many: yet they shall fall by the sword, and by flame, by captivity, and by spoil, many days."

Interpretation: this prophecy continues to talk about the faithful Christians, who taught the true gospel of Jesus Christ to many, but were later captured and killed. In accordance with the other prophecies, that we previously discussed, this is when the true gospel disappeared from earth, and when the apostasy continued to spread around the world. Therefore, nothing existed on earth, which could save mankind from their fallen condition, from that time forward.

Daniel 11:34, "Now when they shall fall, they shall be holpen with a little help: but many shall cleave to them with flatteries."

Interpretation: and then sometime later (many centuries later), after the faithful Christians were killed: **"when they shall fall,"** is when God would send a little help: **"shall be holpen with a little help."**

This **"little help"** arrived on the scene as the "Holy Bible." However, you need to understand that this prophecy is still warning that many ministers would continue to use **"flatteries,"** to build up their individual ministries: **"many shall cleave to them with flatteries."** In other words, the gospel that many ministers would teach, would be corrupted, because many ministers would continue to use **"flatteries"** to build up their individual ministries.

Note: the phrase: **"shall be holpen with a little help,"** is referring to the fact that the Holy Bible arrived on scene, by itself, without a true prophet being sent to teach Christians the correct interpretations. Understand; the phrase: **"shall be holpen with a little help,"** would never have been used, if a true prophet existed on earth, during that time.

> **Daniel 11:35, "And some of them of understanding shall fall, to try them, and to purge, and to make them white, even to the time of the end: because it is yet for a time appointed."**

Interpretation: this verse is now talking about the Christians, who were martyred in the past, and would continue to be martyred, in the future: **"them of understanding shall fall."** We learn from this prophecy, that Christians will continue to be murdered, even during the last days: **"even to the time of the end."** The phrase: **"to make them white,"** is referring to the Christians who would pass the test of faith, which would make them worthy to wear the white garments. We learn more about these white garments in "Revelation:"

> **"Thou hast a few names even in Sardis which have not defiled their garments; and they shall walk with me in white: for they are worthy. HE THAT OVERCOMETH, THE SAME SHALL BE CLOTHED IN WHITE RAIMENT; and I will**

not blot out his name out of the book of life, but I will confess his name before my Father, and before his angels" (Revelation 3:4-5).

"After this I beheld, and, lo, a great multitude, which no man could number, of all nations, and kindreds, and people, and tongues, stood before the throne, and before the Lamb, CLOTHED WITH WHITE ROBES, and palms in their hands" (Revelation 7:9).

Note: this is one thing that the different Christian denominations, do have in common, even without their knowledge. When Christians are martyred, because of their faith in Jesus Christ, their personal sacrifice guarantees that they will receive the highest rewards from God. They will immediately be cleansed, from their sins, which will make them worthy to wear the white garments. Because Jesus shed his blood for us, and because these faithful Christians shed their blood for him, is what makes these Christians so special and worthy to wear the white garments.

"Greater love hath no man than this, that a man lay down his life for his friends" (John 15:13).

Note: from verses 36 through 45, we learn about the entire history of the Roman Empire, and the twelve Caesars who ruled over this empire, from 60 B.C. to 96 A.D.

Daniel 11:36, "And the king shall do according to his will; and he shall exalt himself, and magnify himself above every god, and shall speak marvelous things against the God of gods, and shall prosper till the indignation be accomplished: for that that is determined shall be done."

Interpretation: this verse explains that the different Roman Caesars would continue to do whatever they desired: **"the king shall do according to his will."** The different Caesars often proclaimed that they were superior, to every god that existed, which fulfilled the prophecy: **"and he shall exalt himself, and magnify himself above every god, and shall speak marvelous things against the God of gods, and shall prosper."** This disrespect was predicted to continue until this kingdom comes to an end: **"till the indignation be accomplished."** We also learn, from this prophecy, that these things were scheduled to happen: **"for that that is determined shall be done."**

> **Daniel 11:37, "Neither shall he regard the God of his fathers, nor the desire of women, nor regard any god: for he shall magnify himself above all."**

Interpretation: we learn from this prophecy, that Augustus Caesar did not respect any of the gods, that his forefathers worshipped: **"Neither shall he regard the God of his fathers."** Because he also had no respect for the women explains why he did not listen to any of their desires: **"nor the desire of women."** Because he did not respect any god: **"nor regard any god,"** he would often proclaim that he was superior to every god, that existed: **"For he shall magnify himself above all."**

> **Daniel 11:38, "But in his estate shall he honour the God of forces: and a god whom his fathers knew not shall he honour with gold, with silver, and with precious stones, and pleasant things."**

Interpretation: Augustus Caesar chose to worship the **"God of forces,"** and a different god that his forefathers never worshipped: **"a god whom his fathers knew not."** The **"God of forces,"** is talking about the different gods, who controlled the natural forces on earth, and throughout the universe. For example: Cardea (or Carda) was the wind god; Jupiter was the rain and storm god; Vulcan was the god of fire; Apollo was the sun god; and Luna was the moon god. Augustus Caesar also established that the different Caesars should also be worshipped after their death, and to honor them **"with gold, with silver, and with precious stones, and pleasant things."** In fact, the first Roman Caesar who declared that he was god, was Julius Caesar. Throughout the Roman Empire many different gods were worshipped, and many beautiful temples were built, to honor them.

> **Daniel 11:39, "Thus shall he do in the most strong holds with a strange god, whom he shall acknowledge and increase with glory: and he shall cause them to rule over many, and shall divide the land for gain."**

Interpretation: the different Caesars worshipped many different and strange gods, and would often build beautiful temples to honor them, throughout the Roman Empire: **"god, whom he shall acknowledge and increase with glory."** They also forced many people to worship their Roman gods: **"and he shall cause them to rule over many."** It was also common, for the different Caesars to divide up the conquered lands for money, and for political gain: **"and shall divide the land for gain."**

> **Daniel 11:40, "And at the time of the end shall the king of the south push at him: and the king of the north shall come against him like a whirlwind, with chariots, and with horsemen, and with many ships; and he shall enter into the countries, and shall overflow and pass over."**

Interpretation: the phrase: **"at the time of the end,"** is referring to the "last days" of Judah, Israel, and Jerusalem, after the First Roman Jewish war begins. Understand; the phrase: **"at the time of the end"** is not talking about the "last days" on earth, before Jesus returns. The

"king of the south" is referring to the leader of the Jewish rebellion: Menahem ben Yehuda. This is when Nero, **"the king of the north,"** appointed his son, General Vespasian to take charge of this war. The rest of this prophecy is explaining what happened after the Romans attacked and destroyed Jerusalem, Judah, and Israel. Notice that the Roman soldiers arrived **"with many ships,"** confirming what we previously discussed in verse thirty, which predicted: **"For the ships of Chittim shall come against him."**

Daniel 11:41, "He shall enter also into the glorious land, and many countries shall be overthrown: but these shall escape out of his hand, even Edom, and Moab, and the chief of the children of Ammon."

Interpretation: this verse is talking about the history of the Roman Empire, from 146 B.C. when the Macedonian-Greek Empire was conquered, to when the rule of the twelve Caesars ended, in 96 A.D. The **"glorious land"** is referring to Athens, Greece. Even though the twelve Caesars conquered many different countries, during their existence, their territories did not include the lands of Edom, Moab, or the land of the Ammonites. This scripture wants us to know that even though General Vespasian successfully attacked and conquered Israel, Judah, and Jerusalem, many Israelites were still able to escape from being captured: **"but these shall escape out of his hand,"** by simply fleeing to the land behind the Dead Sea, to the lands of Edom, Moab, and the Ammonites: **"but these shall escape out of his hand, even Edom, and Moab, and the chief of the children of Ammon."**

To prove that this prophecy is not talking about our "latter days," requires that we ask one very important question: "at what point did Edom, Moab, and the chief priests of Ammon escape from being captured?" The answer: "this happened during the reign of the twelve

Caesars, which ended, in 96 A.D." The Edomites were ancient descendants of Esau; the Moabites and Ammonites were ancient descendants of Lot. The fact that the lands of Edom, Moab, and Ammon do not exist, in modern times, provides proof that this prophecy was fulfilled when these lands still existed.

> **Daniel 11:42, "He shall stretch forth his hand also upon the countries: and the land of Egypt shall not escape."**

> **Daniel 11:43, "But he shall have power over the treasures of gold and of silver, and over all the precious things of Egypt: and the Libyans and the Ethiopians shall be at his steps."**

Interpretation: these scriptures are now explaining that the authority of the Roman Empire, during the reign of the twelve Caesars, extended into the land of Egypt, and were at the very steps of Libya and Ethiopia. This scripture is proven true, when you compare this scripture, with a map that shows the territory of the Roman Empire, in 96 A.D. You will also notice that the lands behind the Dead Sea, were not part of the Roman Empire, during that time: Edom, Moab, and Ammon.

> **Daniel 11:44, "But tidings out of the east and out of the north shall trouble him: therefore he shall go forth with great fury to destroy, and utterly to make away many."**

Interpretation: Domitian had to deal with several serious situations, concerning the eastern territories of Pannonia, and the northern territories of Germania, during his reign. In 85 A.D., Domitian received bad news from the northern territories, that the Moesian governor, Oppius Sabinus, was killed. This caused the Dacian war. It was during Domitian's reign, when the "second Dacian war" was also fought, against the German tribes, and when the "first and second Pannonian wars" were fought, against Pannonia. As you can see, during his reign, many people were killed in battle: **"he shall go forth with great fury to destroy, and utterly to make away many."**

Daniel 11:45, "And he shall plant the tabernacles of his palace between the seas in the glorious holy mountain; yet he shall come to his end, and none shall help him."

Interpretation: Domitian was a very religious man, at least from the perspective that he worshipped the Roman gods, which existed during his lifetime. Domitian often claimed that he was directly related to the gods of Minerva and Jupiter. The reference to the **"glorious holy mountain,"** is referring to the Palatine Hill, located in Rome. This was a very sacred hill to the Roman people, because this is where they built the temple of Apollo, and many other beautiful palaces, to honor their gods and the different Caesars they worshipped. This prophecy is letting us know that this is also where Domitian decided to build his palace: **"And he shall plant the tabernacles of his palace between the seas in the glorious holy mountain."** In fact, the ancient ruins of his palace can still be seen, in modern times. The fact that Italy is a peninsula proves that Rome is located between the seas. Even though Domitian was honored, with a palace of his own, nobody intervened to help him from being assassinated: **"yet he shall come to his end, and none shall help him.** He was assassinated, in 96 A.D., which ended the reign of the twelve Caesars. The fact that this prophecy predicted that his palace would be built on a **"glorious holy mountain,"** located **"between the seas,"** provides proof that this prophecy was fulfilled by Domitian, in 96 A.D.

"Book of Daniel" Chapter 8
King James Version

Even though Daniel received the prophecies in this chapter, two years after he received the prophecies in chapter seven, Daniel's prophecies are easier to understand, when they are studied in accordance with the series of events. With this in mind, we will now begin our discussion, with chapter eight:

> **Daniel 8: 1, "In the third year of the reign of king Belshazzar a vision appeared unto me, even unto me Daniel, after that which appeared unto me at the first."**

Interpretation: King Nabonidus, the father of Belshazzar, ruled over Babylon between the years of 556 and 538 B.C. It is interesting to note that some historians claim that Belshazzar was never a king. However, it appears that Daniel disagrees with their opinion, because he claims that he received this vision, during the third-year reign of "King Belshazzar" (554 B.C.) When Daniel says: **"after that which appeared unto me at the first,"** this simply means that Daniel received the prophecies in chapter eight, the same way that he previously received the prophecies in chapter seven: in a dream (see Daniel 7:1).

Daniel 8:2, "And I saw in a vision; and it came to pass, when I saw, that I was at Shushan in the palace, which is in the province of Elam; and I saw in a vision, and I was by the river Ulai."

Interpretation: it appears that Daniel was at the palace in Shushan, in the province of Elam, when he received a vision, that he was standing **"by the river Ulai."**

Daniel 8:3, "Then I lifted up mine eyes, and saw, and, behold, there stood before the river a ram which had two horns: and the two horns were high; but one was higher than the other, and the higher came up last."

Interpretation: the "Ram" represents the "Great Persian Empire." The two horns on the Ram represents the two kings who once ruled over this kingdom together: a Mede and a Persian. When this verse says: **"and the two horns were high,"** it simply means that both kings were very rich. The richest king that came up last: **"and the higher came up last,"** is referring to the last king, who was named "Darius III."

Daniel 8:4, "I saw the ram pushing westward, and northward, and southward; so that no beasts might stand before him, neither was there any that could deliver out of his hand; but he did according to his will, and became great."

Interpretation: the "Persian Empire" had a very powerful military, and successfully conquered a vast amount of territory, during its existence. No other kingdom (**"no beasts"**) could stop the Persian Empire from expanding its territory: **"neither was there any that could deliver out of his hand."** The Ram **"did according to his will and became great,"** which became known, as the "Great Persian Empire."

Daniel 8:5, "And as I was considering, behold, an he goat came from the west on the face of the whole earth, and touched not the ground: and the goat had a notable horn between his eyes."

Interpretation: the **"he Goat"** that **"came from the west,"** is referring to "Alexander the Great," when he ruled over the "Macedonian-Greek Empire," which was located west of Persia. He successfully conquered the "Great Persian Empire" in approximately ten years. The phrase **"and touched not the ground,"** is referring to just how fast "Alexander the Great" defeated the Persian armies, in battle. In other words, the Persian armies were defeated so fast, that the feet of the Macedonians did not even have time to touch the ground. The notable horn, which was set between the eyes of the goat, represents "Alexander the Great," who focused his eyes on conquering the "Great Persian Empire," during his lifetime.

Daniel 8:6, "And he came to the ram that had two horns, which I had seen standing before the river, and ran unto him in the fury of his power."

Interpretation: the first battle was fought on the banks of the Granicus River in 334 B.C. This is when Alexander attacked the powerful army, of the "Great Persian Empire," and won: **"and ran unto him in the fury of his power."**

Note: it needs to be understood that **"two kings"** did not rule over the "Great Persian Empire," during the time, when "Alexander the Great" attacked this empire. Therefore, the reference to the **"two kings"** is to let us know that this is the same empire, which was once ruled by the Medes and the Persians, together. The Persian Empire defeated the Median Empire in 550 B.C., which was 216 years before "Alexander the Great" fought the first battle, against the Persians, in 334 B.C.

Daniel 8:7, "And I saw him come close unto the ram, and he was moved with choler against him, and smote the ram, and break his two horns: and there was no power in the ram to stand before him, but he cast him down to the ground, and stamped upon him: and there was none that could deliver the ram out of his hand."

Interpretation: "Alexander the Great" successfully defeated the "Great Persian Empire" (**"the ram"**), in about ten years, but continued to pursue "Darius III." As a result, "Darius III" successfully raised another Persian army, which was also defeated by "Alexander." Because Alexander had no respect for Darius III, he refused to accept any peace agreements that "Darius III," offered: fulfilling the prophecy: **"he cast him down to the ground, and stamped upon him."** During that time, no army existed, which could have stopped "Alexander the Great" from defeating the "Great Persian Empire," which fulfilled the prophecy: **"and there was none that could deliver the ram out of his hand."** Alexander was denied the opportunity to kill "Darius III," because he was eventually murdered by his own cousin, Bessus.

Daniel 8:8, "Therefore the he goat waxed very great: and when he was strong, the great horn was broken; and for it came up four notable ones toward the four winds of heaven."

Interpretation: the "Macedonian-Greek Empire," became a very powerful kingdom, under the rule of "Alexander the Great." However, after his death, when **"the great horn was broken,"** is when this kingdom was divided up, among his powerful generals. As a result, this kingdom eventually evolved into four powerful dynasties, referred to as the **"four notable ones,"** which also divided this kingdom **"toward the four winds of heaven."** The names of these four powerful Dynasties were: the Antigonid Dynasty, the Ptolemaic Dynasty, the Seleucid Dynasty, and the Attalid Dynasty.

> **Daniel 8:9, "And out of one of them came forth a little horn, which waxed exceeding great, toward the south, and toward the east, and toward the pleasant land."**

Interpretation: we are now being informed, that at some point, another powerful leader (a **"little horn"**) would rise to power, from within one of these divided territories: **"out of one of them."** This prophecy began to be fulfilled, long after Macedonia became a Roman province, in 146 B.C. Several years later (60 B.C.), Julius Caesar arrived on the scene (the **"little horn"**), who made the "Roman Republic" into a great military force. This prophecy also predicts that the Roman Republic would eventually expand its territories to include **"the pleasant land"** of Israel, Judea, and Jerusalem.

Note: it needs to be remembered that **"the glorious land"** is referring to Athens, while **"the pleasant land"** is now referring to Israel, Judea, and Jerusalem.

> **Daniel 8:10, "And it waxed great, even to the host of heaven; and it cast down some of the host and of the stars to the ground, and stamped upon them."**

Interpretation: the Roman Republic soon became a very powerful kingdom: **"And it waxed great."** The Roman citizens worshiped many different gods, including the planets, and the stars. The fact that the different Caesars would often proclaim that they were superior to every god that existed, is what dishonored the Roman gods, and **"brought them down to the ground and stamped on them."**

> **Daniel 8:11, "Yea, he magnified himself even to the prince of the host, and by him the daily sacrifice was taken away,**

and the place of his sanctuary was cast down."

Interpretation: this verse is explaining that the Roman Caesars authority, would eventually extend to Jerusalem, and under his authority Pontius Pilate (the host) would then be appointed as governor, over Judea (Luke 3:1). The **"prince of the host"** is referring to Jesus and Pontius Pilate. Pontius Pilate was the **"host,"** who presided over the trial of Jesus, while Jesus was the **"prince."** The prophecy, concerning the **"daily sacrifice was taken away"** is referring to the crucifixion of Jesus, which permanently abolished the daily animal blood sacrifices, for the remission of sins. Therefore, the blood of Jesus is what washes away our sins, today. The prophecy: **"and the place of his sanctuary was cast down,"** is referring to the temple in Jerusalem, when the Romans destroyed the temple, in 70 A.D.

Daniel 8:12, "And an host was given him against the daily sacrifice by reason of transgression, and it cast down the truth to the ground; and it practiced and prospered."

Interpretation: this verse is talking about the trial of Jesus. Pontius Pilate was the **"host,"** who listened to the false charges, filed against Jesus: the **"reason of transgression."** The false charges in this trial, **"cast down the truth to the ground,"** because the false charges **"practiced and prospered,"** which caused Jesus to be crucified. The fact that the crucifixion of Jesus abolished the daily sacrifices, for the remission of sins, is why this verse is using the phrase: **"against the daily sacrifice."**

Daniel 8:13, "Then I heard one saint speaking, and another saint said unto that certain saint which spake, How long shall be the vision concerning the daily sacrifice, and the transgression of desolation, to give both the sanctuary and the host to be trodden under foot?"

Interpretation: one saint is simply asking another saint a question: **"How long shall be the vision concerning the daily sacrifice, and the transgression of desolation, to give both the sanctuary and the host to be trodden under foot?"** The phrase: **"the vision concerning the daily sacrifice"** is referring to the crucifixion of Jesus. While **"the transgression of desolation to give both the sanctuary and the host to be trodden under foot?"** is referring to the apostasy, which would spread around the world, after the temple in Jerusalem is destroyed. Therefore, this means that **"both the sanctuary and the host"** would begin to be **"trodden under foot"** (disrespected), after the temple in Jerusalem is destroyed. In simple language, one saint was simply asking the other saint this question: "how long will the worldwide apostasy remain on earth, which allows **"both the sanctuary and the host to be trodden under foot?"**

> **Daniel 8:14, "And he said unto me, Unto two thousand and three hundred days; then shall the sanctuary be cleansed."**

Interpretation: the other saint then explains that in 2300 days (years), from some unspecified date, the sanctuary would then be cleansed: **"then shall the sanctuary be cleansed."** In other words, the worldwide apostasy was scheduled to end, after Daniel's **"sanctuary be cleansed"** prophecy is fulfilled.

Note: we talked about this prophecy, earlier, in more detail.

> **Daniel 8:15, "And it came to pass, when I, even I Daniel, had seen the vision, and sought for the meaning, then, behold, there stood before me as the appearance of a man."**

Interpretation: this is when Angel Gabriel appeared.

> **Daniel 8:16, "And I heard a man's voice between the banks**

of Ulai, which called, and said, Gabriel, make this man to understand the vision."

Interpretation: Daniel then heard another voice, instructing Gabriel to explain the vision, to Daniel.

Daniel 8:17, "So he came near where I stood: and when he came, I was afraid, and fell upon my face: but he said unto me, Understand, O son of man: for at the time of the end shall be the vision."

Interpretation: when Gabriel first approached Daniel, Daniel became afraid, and fell upon his face. Shortly thereafter, Gabriel begins to explain that the "sanctuary be cleansed" prophecy would be fulfilled, sometime during the last days: **"for at the time of the end shall be the vision."**

Daniel 8:18, "Now as he was speaking with me, I was in a deep sleep on my face toward the ground: but he touched me, and set me upright."

Interpretation: Daniel explains that he was in a deep sleep when Gabriel first began to speak. Gabriel then touches Daniel and he sat up.

Daniel 8:19, "And he said, Behold, I will make thee know what shall be in the last end of the indignation: for at the time appointed the end shall be."

Interpretation: behold, I will now explain the different visions, which you were previously shown: **"in the last end of the indignation."** Gabriel is talking about the prophecies, which Daniel received, in verses 3 through 12. The **"indignation,"** is referring to the terrible treatment, which Jesus was predicted to suffer, as explained in verse

12. Gabriel then explains, how the prophecies would be fulfilled in the order that Daniel was shown, and how each powerful kingdom (referring to the Great Persian Empire and the Macedonian-Greek Empire) would come to power, and rule for an appointed amount of time. And then each powerful kingdom would come to an end: **"for at the time appointed the end shall be."**

Note: many ministers misinterprets this prophecy because they contend that: **"in the last end of the indignation"** and **"for at the time appointed the end shall be,"** provides proof that these prophecies will be fulfilled, sometime during the last days. However, as you can plainly see, these prophecies were fulfilled, many centuries before we were born.

Angel Gabriel then explains these same prophecies, to Daniel, again.

> **Daniel 8:20, "The ram which thou sawest having two horns are the kings of Media and Persia."**

Interpretation (compare verse 3): Gabriel explains that the **"two horns,"** represent the two kings who once ruled from within, the "Great Persian Empire." The fact that the "Great Persian Empire" was defeated by "Alexander the Great," in 330 B.C., proves that this prophecy is not talking about our "last days."

> **Daniel 8:21, "And the rough goat is the king of Grecia: and the great horn that is between his eyes is the first king."**

Interpretation (compare verse 5): the **"rough goat,"** is referring to the "Macedonian-Greek Empire" (Grecia), with "Alexander the Great" as the king. It was Phillip II who originally created this empire through the different treaties and agreements that he made. He focused his eyes on conquering the "Great Persian Empire," but was assassinated, in

336 B.C. It was "Alexander the Great" who successfully conquered the "Great Persian Empire."

> **Daniel 8:22, "Now that being broken, whereas four stood up for it, four kingdoms shall stand up out of the nation, but not in his power."**

Interpretation (compare verse 8): **"Now that being broken,"** is referring to the death of "Alexander the Great," in 323 B.C. This is when the "Macedonian-Greek Empire" was divided up, among his powerful generals: **"whereas four stood up for it, four kingdoms shall stand up out of the nation."** The four kingdoms are the four powerful dynasties, which eventually came to power, after this kingdom was divided up. The phrase: **"but not in his power,"** is simply predicting that after the death of "Alexander the Great," the "Macedonian-Greek Empire" would never be unified under one powerful leader, again.

> **Daniel 8:23, "And in the latter time of their kingdom, when the transgressors are come to the full, a king of fierce countenance, and understanding dark sentences, shall stand up."**

Note: this is another verse that many ministers continue to misinterpret. It needs to be understood that this verse is not talking about our "latter days."

Interpretation (compare verse 9): when this verse says: **"in the latter time OF THEIR KINGDOM,"** this is referring to the latter time (or the last days) of the "Macedonian-Greek Empire." The phrase: **"when the transgressors are come to the full,"** is referring to the time, after the four powerful dynasties are created. This verse is simply letting us know that **"in the latter time of their kingdom:"** after the Macedonian kingdom is divided up, the four kingdoms will also be conquered, when another powerful leader by the name of Augustus Caesar will arrive on the scene as: **"a king of fierce countenance, and understanding dark sentences."** This is when the Roman Empire will take its turn in power as the fourth kingdom.

Daniel 8:24, "And his power shall be mighty, but not by his own power; and he shall destroy wonderfully, and shall prosper, and practise, and shall destroy the mighty and the holy people."

Interpretation (compare verses 10-11): it was the Roman Senate who gave the power to the different Caesars: **"not by his own power."** During the reign of these different Caesars, the Holy Roman Empire prospered, and became very powerful. This kingdom successfully conquered many **"mighty"** and powerful kingdoms, which also included the territories of Israel, Judea, and Jerusalem: **"the holy people."** The different Caesars destroyed **"wonderfully,"** because they would often celebrate their military conquests, by throwing magnificent and wonderful parties.

Daniel 8:25, "And through his policy also he shall cause craft to prosper in his hand; and he shall magnify himself in his heart, and by peace shall destroy many: he shall also stand up against Prince of princes; but he shall be broken without hand."

Interpretation (compare verse 12): it is a fact that the Roman Empire prospered during the reign of the different Caesars: **"And through his policy also he shall cause craft to prosper in his hand."** These different Caesars would often proclaim that they were superior to every god that existed: **"he shall magnify himself in his heart."** It was during the time of peace, when the different Caesars would build beautiful temples, to honor their gods. They would also force the conquered nations to worship them. It was this practice, during the time of **"peace,"** which spiritually **"destroyed many."** It was Tiberius Caesar who stood up: **"stand up against Prince of princes,"** because under his authority, is when Jesus was crucified. Tiberius Caesar spent his final days in seclusion, and died in 37 A.D., fulfilling the prophecy: **"he shall be broken without hand."** He fulfilled this prophecy, because he died of natural causes, and was not assassinated or killed in battle.

Daniel 8:26, "And the vision of the evening and the morning which was told is true: wherefore shut thou up the vision; for it shall be for many days."

Interpretation: Gabriel then explains to Daniel that both visions, that he received, are true. Daniel received the first vision (verses 2 through 14) in the morning: and received the second vision (verses 15 through 25), in the evening. Daniel was then told not to worry about these prophecies, because they were not scheduled to be fulfilled, until many years in the very distant future: **"wherefore shut thou up the vision; for it shall be for many days."**

Note: when Daniel was told: **"wherefore shut thou up the vision; for it shall be for many days,"** this simply meant that these prophecies were not scheduled to be fulfilled, until sometime in the distant future, from Daniel's perspective. This statement does not prove that these prophecies were scheduled to be fulfilled during our "last days." In fact, when you study these prophecies, you can plainly see that these prophecies were fulfilled, many centuries before we were born. Also notice that nothing, in these prophecies, mentions anything about some future anti-Christ, who will make his appearance on earth, during the "last days." Many modern-day ministers have taken the verse, which says: **"And in the latter time of their kingdom, when the transgressors are come to the full, a king of fierce countenance, and understanding dark sentences, shall stand up"** (Daniel 8:23), and then added several other verses from Daniel, chapter 11, to provide proof that Daniel was talking about some future anti-Christ. The sad fact remains, that the different (and very evil) Caesars who ruled over the Roman Empire, fulfilled these prophecies. However, Daniel does talk about several other important prophecies, which were scheduled to be fulfilled, during the "last days."

This is where Daniel, chapter 7, comes into play.

"Book of Daniel" Chapter 7
King James Version

Daniel 7:1, "In the first year of Belshazzar king of Babylon Daniel had a dream and visions of his head upon his bed: then he wrote the dream, and told the sum of the matters."

INTERPRETATION: DANIEL RECEIVED the visions (or prophecies) in this chapter, in a dream, which he immediately wrote down. Daniel received these prophecies, in 556 B.C., during the first year of Belshazzar. This proves that he received these prophecies two years, before he received the prophecies that we previously discussed, in chapter eight.

Note: the reason why this chapter is being discussed, after Chapter 8, is because the following prophecies teaches more about Nebuchadnezzar's dream, which we previously discussed:

Daniel 7:2, "Daniel spake and said, I saw in my vision by night, and, behold, the four winds of the heaven strove upon the great sea."

Daniel 7:3, "And four great beasts came up from the sea, diverse one from another."

Interpretation: Daniel sees four great, and diverse kingdoms, which would eventually come to power: referred to as the **"four great beasts."**

Daniel 7:4, "The first was like a lion, and had eagle's wings: I beheld till the wings thereof were plucked, and it was lifted up from the earth, and made stand upon the feet as a man, and a man's heart was given to it."

Interpretation: the lion represents the Babylonian Empire. The **"wings"** of this kingdom were **"plucked,"** and **"lifted up from the earth,"** after the death of Nebuchadnezzar. This is when the power of this kingdom was greatly diminished. The next king, who followed Nebuchadnezzar, was Nabonidus: the father of Belshazzar. Because Nabonidus did not have any relationship with God, also meant that he would not receive any help or protection, from God. Therefore, the future of Babylon was completely in his hands: **"and made stand upon the feet as a man, and a man's heart was given to it."**

Daniel 7:5, "And behold another beast, a second, like to a bear, and it raised up itself on one side, and it had three ribs in the mouth of it between the teeth of it: and they said thus unto it, Arise, devour much flesh."

Interpretation: this second kingdom, represented by the bear, is referring to the "Great Persian Empire." Because this second kingdom was once governed by two separate kings; a Mede and a Persian, with one being more powerful than the other, is why we see this bear: **"raised up itself on one side."** This bear is out of balance, because the leadership of this kingdom, was also out of balance. The three ribs, in the mouth of the bear, represent the three continents that the "Great Persian Empire" occupied, during its existence: part of Asia, part of Africa, and part of Europe.

Daniel 7:6, "After this I beheld, and lo another, like a leopard, which had upon the back of it four wings of a fowl; the beast had also four heads; and dominion was given to it."

Interpretation: the leopard represents the "Macedonian-Greek Empire," which became very powerful, under the leadership of "Alexander the Great." After his death, this third kingdom was then divided up, among his powerful generals, which continued to conquer many other nations: **"and dominion was given to it."** When this prophecy says: **"the beast had also four heads,"** this is referring to the four powerful dynasties, which eventually evolved from the Macedonian-Greek Empire: the Antigonid Dynasty; the Ptolemaic Dynasty; the Seleucid Dynasty; and the Attalid Dynasty.

Daniel 7:7, "After this I saw in the night visions, and behold a fourth beast, dreadful and terrible, and strong exceedingly; and it had great iron teeth: it devoured and brake in pieces, and stamped the residue with the feet of it: and it was diverse from all the beasts that were before it; and it had ten horns."

Interpretation: this fourth beast is the "Roman Republic;" the "Roman Empire;" the "Holy Roman Empire;" and the "Holy Roman Empire of the German Nation." Some historians claim that the "Holy Roman Empire" did not exist, until after Charlemagne was crowned, in 800 A.D. There are others who claim that the "Holy Roman Empire" did not exist, until after "King Conrad I" was crowned, in 911. In either case, both theories contradict Daniel's prophecies, because Daniel explains that it was Augustus Caesar who became the first "Holy Roman Emperor," as soon as he accepted his religious title of "Augustus" ("the exalted one"). Because Augustus was a religious title, historians should have recognized the Roman Republic as a religious kingdom, from that time forward. It is a fact that the "Holy Roman Empire" was **"dreadful and terrible, and strong exceedingly."** This empire was the most **"diverse"** kingdom on earth, simply because it was comprised of many different races, languages, and cultures. The **"ten horns"** represent the "ten kings," who ruled from within the "Holy Roman Empire," as the "League of the Rhine." This league was originally created, in 1658, which consisted of several powerful Monarchs and Princes.

Note: before continuing, it needs to be understood that Daniel does not pull any punches, when he talks about this fourth kingdom. Therefore, Catholics who desire not to hear anything negative about their church, or the Pope, should not read this chapter beyond this point. It needs to be understood that I did not write the "Book of Daniel" or "The Book of Revelation." I am only explaining how to recognize and decipher the hidden clues, which reveal exactly when and how these prophecies, were fulfilled. Even though I do offer my opinion, concerning how these prophecies should be deciphered (and interpreted), the readers must still decide (for themselves) if the correct interpretations were achieved, or not. Do these interpretations match the hidden clues that we uncovered? If these interpretations can pass this test, then you can rest assured that the correct interpretations, were achieved.

In 1806, Napoleon made some political agreements with the kings and princes in the "League of the Rhine," and then renamed this newly formed organization the "Confederation of the Rhine." This is when the next prophecy comes into play:

> **Daniel 7:8,** "I considered the horns, and, behold, there came up among them another little horn, before whom there were three of the first horns plucked up by the roots: and, behold, in this horn were eyes like the eyes of man, and a mouth speaking great things."

Interpretation: when Daniel says that he **"considered the horns,"** this means that he considered the role that the different kings, within the "Confederation of the Rhine" would play, sometime in the future (the future from his perspective). We learn that **"another little horn,"** was scheduled to come to power, from within the "Confederation of the Rhine," shortly after three other horns are defeated in battle: **"plucked up by the roots."** The words **"before whom"** plays an important role in understanding this prophecy. This prophecy is saying that three kings will be defeated, **before** this second **"little horn,"** will come to power. We are also informed that in the administration, of this **"little horn,"** there will be a powerful individual who will have **"the eyes of man, and a mouth speaking great things."** Understand: the first **"little horn"** was Augustus Caesar. This second **"little horn"** was not scheduled to arrive on the scene, until sometime after 1806, after the "Confederation of the Rhine" is created. Therefore, this timetable proves that this second **"little horn"** was William Frederick Louis (William I or Wilhelm I). The powerful individual who worked from within his administration, who had the **"the eyes of man, and a mouth speaking great things"** was his Prime Minister, Otto Von Bismarck.

When this prophecy is compared with the historical record, we discover that in 1512, the name of the "Holy Roman Empire" was officially changed to the "Holy Roman Empire of the German Nation." Notice that this name change occurred, long before the "League of the Rhine" was created, in 1658. Therefore, when Napoleon defeated the "Holy Roman Empire" in battle, in 1805, he actually defeated the "Holy Roman Empire of the German Nation." This was the empire that was completely dissolved in August 1806. And then in July 1806, the "Confederation of the Rhine" was created, and this is when the "ten kings" began to rule, from within the "Kingdom of Clay" (the "First French Empire"). It needs to be understood that even though the "Confederation of the Rhine" was abolished in 1813, after Napoleon was defeated in the battle of Leipzig, these kings remained in power until after the European Revolutions ended, in 1848. In 1861, William Frederick Louis (William I or Wilhelm I) became the King of Prussia (Germany), and chose Otto Von Bismarck as his Prime Minister. Bismarck used the wars to unite the German Nations. The three nations, who were defeated in battle, which fulfilled the prophecy: **"there were three of the first horns plucked up by the roots"** were: Denmark in 1866; Austria in 1866; and France in 1871.

In 1871, William Frederick Louis (William I or Wilhelm I) became the first German Emperor, after he resurrected the "Holy Roman Empire of the German Nation" from the ashes of military defeat. This is when the "Second Reich" arrived on the scene, which was also referred to as the "Second Realm," or the "Second Empire." After the "Second Reich" was defeated, in WWI, it was dissolved in 1918. Because the "Second Reich" was dissolved after WWI, should help people understand why Adolph Hitler desired to create the "Third Reich," during WWII. Hitler wanted to become the next "German Emperor" of the "Holy Roman Empire of the German Nation."

Otto Von Bismarck wrote the constitution for the "North German Confederation," which was officially adopted on July 1, 1867. Precisely 42 months later, on Jan 12, 1871, "Wilhelm I of Prussia" (William Frederick Louis) officially became the first German Emperor of the "Holy Roman Empire of the German Nation." The fact that the "North German Confederation" lasted for a total of 42 months, provides proof that this is the kingdom, which is mentioned in the "Book of Revelation" (Revelation 13:5). These 42 months were provided as a clue, to let us know that the "resurrected" fourth kingdom, would be the "Holy Roman Empire of the German Nation."

This is where the prophecy, concerning the two heads, come into play: **"And I saw one of his heads as it were wounded to death; and his deadly wound was healed: and all the world wondered**

after the beast (Revelation 13:3). This scripture is talking about the "Two Headed Black Eagle," which represented the "Holy Roman Empire," for many centuries. Two events caused one of its heads to be wounded to death: the first event is when Napoleon defeated the "Holy Roman Empire of the German Nation" in battle: the second event is when the "Holy Roman Empire of the German Nation" was dissolved in 1806. The second part of this prophecy, concerning: **"and its deadly wound was healed"** (Revelation 13:3), was fulfilled in 1870, when Pope Pius IX officially announced that the Roman Catholic Church was the Roman Republic. This deadly wound was healed for a second time, in 1871, after the "Holy Roman Empire of the German Nation" was resurrected, as the "Second Reich." Therefore, this resurrected fourth kingdom was ruled by two powerful leaders: one was a powerful religious leader, while the other was a powerful, secular leader. After WWI, the "Holy Roman Empire of the German Nation" was dissolved, which is when Keiser Wilhelm II resigned his position as the German Emperor.

However, the resignation of Keiser Wilhelm II did not change the fact that the "Holy Roman Empire" would remain, on earth, through the hands of the "Holy Roman Catholic Church." It would be this church, which would fulfill the third part of the prophecy in Revelation, that reads: **"and all the world wondered after the beast"** (Revelation 13:3). Because the "Roman Republic" is the fourth "beast," and because the "Holy Roman Catholic Church" is still the Roman Republic, proves that this church is the resurrected fourth "beast," mentioned in Daniel's prophecy. The reference to the "dragon," who gave power to this beast: **"And they worshipped the dragon which gave power unto the beast"** (Revelation 13:4), is referring to the Pope, himself.

In 1356, the constitutional structure of the "Holy Roman Empire" was changed, when the "Golden Bull" was adopted. This empowered "seven electors" to choose who the next "Holy Roman Emperor" should be. This agreement was made, hoping that this would eliminate papal interference, in German political affairs. After these "seven electors" choose who the next Emperor should be, this chosen individual would then become the next official "Holy Roman Emperor," after he is crowned by the Pope. Therefore, this "Holy Roman Emperor" received his power, and great authority, from the hands of the Pope: **"and the dragon gave him his power, and his seat, and great authority"** (Revelation 13:2).

With this understanding, will now return to Daniel, chapter 7:

Daniel 7:9, "I beheld till the thrones were cast down, and the Ancient of days did sit, whose garment was white as snow, and the hair of his head like the pure wool: his throne was like the fiery flame, and his wheels as burning fire."

Interpretation: we learn from this prophecy, that the "Holy Roman Empire" will remain on earth, until the judgment begins. This prophecy becomes easier to understand, after we add some missing information, to this prophecy:

"I beheld (the "Holy Roman Empire") till the thrones were cast down, and the Ancient of days ("Michael the Archangel") did sit, whose garment was white as snow, and the hair of his head like the pure wool: his throne was like the fiery flame, and his wheels as burning fire" (Daniel 7:9).

Sadly, most modern-day bible scholars do not understand that the **"Ancient of days,"** is another name for Adam. Adam is the **"Ancient of days,"** because he was the first man, on earth. In the preexistence, before the earth was created, Adam was also "Michael the Archangel." This verse is explaining that the "Holy Roman Empire" will remain on earth, until "Michael the Archangel" returns, to begin the judgment. Understand; the "Holy Roman Empire of the German Nation" was dissolved in 1806, and it was dissolved again in 1918, but the "Holy Roman Empire" still remains on earth, today, through the hands of the "Holy Roman Catholic Church."

> **Daniel 7:10, "A fiery stream issued and came forth from before him: thousand thousands ministered unto him, and ten thousand times ten thousand stood before him: the judgment was set, and the books were opened."**

Interpretation: this verse is explaining what will happen during the first resurrection before the judgment begins. This is when millions of angels will arrive, on earth, to minister unto "Michael the Archangel." This is also when billions of people will stand before Michael, to be judged, and when the books will be opened.

Note: we learn more from the "Book of Revelation," which also talks about this judgment, and confirms what we just discussed:

> **"And I saw an ANGEL come down from heaven, having the key of the bottomless pit and a great chain in his hand. And he laid hold on the dragon, that old serpent, which is the Devil, and Satan, and bound him a thousand years, And cast him into the bottomless pit, and shut him up, and set a seal upon him, that he should deceive the nations no more, till the thousand years should be fulfilled: and after that he must be loosed a little season And I saw thrones, and they sat upon them, and judgment was given unto them: and I saw the souls of them that were beheaded for the witness of Jesus, and for the word of God, and which had not worshipped the beast, neither his image, neither had received his mark upon their foreheads, or in their hands;**

and they lived and reigned with Christ a thousand years. But the rest of the dead lived not again until the thousand years were finished. This is the first resurrection" (Revelation 20:1-5).

When studying the "Book of Daniel" (Daniel 7:10) we discovered that this angel is "Michael the Archangel." Also notice that these scriptures prove that these events will take place during **"the first resurrection."**

Daniel 7:11, "I beheld then because of the voice of the great words which the horn spake: I beheld even till the beast was slain, and his body destroyed, and given to the burning flame."

Interpretation: the reference to **"the great words WHICH THE HORN SPAKE,"** in this prophecy, is now talking about a completely different "horn" (a third "horn"), who would rule from within the "Roman Republic," during the "last days." Understand: the **"great words which the horn spake,"** in this prophecy, is not talking about any words previously spoken by Otto Von Bismarck. This is because Bismarck was not a **"little horn,"** but was simply a powerful individual, who worked within the administration of a **"little horn."** This second **"little horn"** was William Frederick Louis. In this prophecy, we are now being told that a third "horn" will rise to power, who will speak great words: the **"great words which the horn spake."** Also notice that this third "horn" will remain in power **"till the beast was slain, and his body destroyed, and given to the burning flame."** The fact that William Frederick Louis died in 1888, and Otto Von Bismarck died in 1898, provides proof that neither of these men fulfilled this prophecy. Because the "Holy Roman Empire of the German Nation" was dissolved, in 1918, also proves that this is not the "Holy Roman Empire" of the "last days." The **"great words"** mentioned in this prophecy, is talking about the false religious doctrines, which would be taught on earth: **"till the beast was slain, and his body destroyed, and given to the burning flame."** The first "horn" was Augustus Caesar; the second "horn" was William Frederick Louis (William I or Wilhelm I); while this third "horn" is a very powerful religious leader, who would rule over the "Roman Republic," from within the "Holy Roman Catholic Church." Therefore, this "third horn" is the Pope, himself.

> **Daniel 7:12; "As concerning the rest of the beasts, they had their dominion taken away: yet their lives were prolonged for a season and time."**

Interpretation: this verse explains that even though the other kingdoms were eventually defeated, in battle: **"they had their dominion taken away,"** these kingdoms still ruled over their individual territories, for a long time: **"their lives were prolonged for a season and time."**

> **Daniel 7:13, "I saw in the night visions, and, behold, one like the Son of man came with the clouds of heaven, and came to the Ancient of days, and they brought him near before him."**

Interpretation: Daniel is now explaining that he had another dream: **"I saw in the night visions."** This is when he saw the **"Son of man"** (Jesus Christ), returning to earth: **"came with the clouds of heaven."** The angels then escorted Jesus to "Michael the Archangel," meaning: **"they brought him near before him.** It needs to be understood that "Michael the Archangel" is the **"Ancient of days."**

> **Daniel 7:14, "And there was given him dominion, and glory, and a kingdom, that all people, nations, and languages, should serve him: his dominion is an everlasting dominion, which shall not pass away, and his kingdom that which shall not be destroyed."**

Interpretation: **after** this judgment is completed, Jesus Christ will then begin his millennial rule, on earth. In accordance with the "Book of Revelation," we are told that the other dead will not resurrect, until after a thousand years have passed:

"But the rest of the dead lived not again until the thousand years were finished." This is the first resurrection" (Revelation 20:5).

Therefore, as you can see, it would be very important to be resurrected, during this first resurrection.

Note: this is the end of the prophecies, which Daniel received, concerning the events that will happen on earth. Because Daniel did not understand these prophecies, he then asks for help, so that he can understand when and how these prophecies would be fulfilled. The following scriptures are a very condensed version for what we previously discussed.

Daniel 7:15, "I Daniel was grieved in my spirit in the midst of my body, and the visions of my head troubled me."

Interpretation: Daniel was greatly troubled by these prophecies, because he did not fully understand what they meant, or when these prophecies were scheduled to be fulfilled. He then asks (in the next verse) that these prophecies be explained to him, again.

Daniel 7:16, "I came near unto one of them that stood by, and asked him the truth of all this. So he told me, and made me know the interpretation of the things."

Interpretation: this is when Daniel approaches another saint, and asks for help, so that he can learn what these prophecies predicted.

Note: keep in mind that the following scriptures, are a very condensed version for the prophecies, that we just discussed, from verses 1 through 14. Therefore, these prophecies are not new prophecies.

This other saint begins to explain:

> **Daniel 7:17, "These great beasts, which are four, are four kings, which shall arise out of the earth."**

Interpretation (compare verse 3): the four beasts, and the four kings, are four kingdoms: the "Babylonian Empire;" the "Persian Empire;" the "Macedonian Greek Empire;" and the "Holy Roman Empire."

> **Daniel 7:18, "But the saints of the most High shall take the kingdom, and possess the kingdom forever, even forever and ever."**

Interpretation: after the "Kingdom of God" is established, on earth, and after the first resurrection is completed, the saints of the **"most High"** (the most High God) will possess the "Kingdom of God," on earth, **"even forever and ever."**

> **Daniel 7:19, "Then I would know the truth of the fourth beast, which was diverse from all the others, exceeding dreadful, whose teeth were of iron, and his nails of brass; which devoured, brake in pieces, and stamped the residue with his feet;"**

Interpretation (compare verse 7): sometime after the "Kingdom of God" is established, on earth, the world will then learn the identity of this fourth beast. This fourth beast is the same beast, which conquered many different kingdoms, during its existence: **"which devoured, brake in pieces, and stamped the residue with his feet."** The "teeth

of iron" represents the "Roman Republic," while the **"nails of brass"** represents the "Macedonian-Greek Empire," after it became a Roman province, in 146 B.C. The reference: **"and stamped the residue with his feet,"** is referring to the "Holy Roman Catholic Church," and the doctrine that this church teaches around the world.

> Daniel 7:20, "And of the ten horns that were in his head, and of the other which came up, and before whom three fell; even of that horn that had eyes, and a mouth that spake very great things, whose look was more stout than his fellows."

Interpretation (compare verse 8): this prophecy predicts that another "horn" will rise to power from within the "League of the Rhine." This: **"and the other which came up,"** is referring to the King of Prussia (William I) before the "North German Confederation" was created, in 1867. The three nations that **"fell,"** were the three nations defeated in battle, by the individual who **"had eyes, and a mouth that spake very great things,"** and **"whose look was more stout than his fellows."** Otto Von Bismarck fulfilled the prophecy: **"whose look was more stout than his fellows"** because he was also known as the "Iron Chancellor."

> Daniel 7:21, "I beheld, and the same horn made war with the saints, and prevailed against them;"

Interpretation (compare verse 11): when this verse says: **"and the same horn,"** this is talking about the third "horn," who will make war with the saints, and prevail against them: **"made war with the saints, and prevailed against them."** This third "horn" is the Pope, who is a very powerful religious leader, in the "Holy Roman Catholic Church."

> Daniel 7:22, "Until the Ancient of days came, and judgment was given to the saints of the most High; and the time came that the saints possessed the kingdom."

Interpretation: this church will remain, on earth, until the **"Ancient of days"** ("Michael the Archangel") arrives, to begin the judgment during the first resurrection. After this judgment is completed, is when the saints will possess the "Kingdom of God," on earth, forever.

We learn more about this "fourth beast" in the "Book of Revelation."

> **"And I saw one of his heads as it were wounded to death; and his deadly wound was healed: and all the world wondered after the beast. And they worshipped the dragon which gave power unto the beast: and they worshipped the beast, saying, Who is like unto the beast? who is able to make war with him? And there was given unto him a mouth speaking great things and blasphemies; and power was given unto him to continue forty and two months"** (Revelation 13:3-5).

When this prophecy says: **"And I saw one of his heads as it were wounded to death;"** this was fulfilled when the fourth kingdom was defeated in battle, by Napoleon Bonaparte in 1805, and when it was completely dissolved in 1806. The prophecy: **"and his deadly wound was healed,"** was fulfilled in 1871, after the "Holy Roman Empire of the German Nation" was resurrected after its military defeat in 1805. The prophecy: **"and all the world wondered after the beast"** is referring to the "Holy Roman Catholic Church." The prophecy: **"And they worshipped the dragon** is referring to the Pope. The prophecy: **"which gave power unto the beast:"** is talking about the Pope who gives power to the "beast," which is the "Holy Roman Catholic Church." The prophecy: **"and they worshipped the beast, saying, Who is like unto the beast? who is able to make war with him?** is referring to the fourth kingdom, which was both the "Holy Roman Catholic Church," and the "Holy Roman Empire of the German Nation." The prophecy: **"And there was given unto him a mouth speaking great things and blasphemies;** is referring to the Pope, who rules over this fourth kingdom, today: the "Holy Roman Catholic Church." The fact that blasphemies is a religious term proves that this prophecy is talking about the Pope. When this prophecy says: **"and power was given unto him to continue forty and two months,"** this is talking about the "North German Confederation," which lasted for a total of 42 months. It was the creation of this German confederation, which made it possible for the "Holy Roman Empire of the German Nation" to be resurrected, in 1871.

Note: the 42 months began July 1, 1867, when the Constitution for the "North German Confederation" was officially adopted. These 42 months ended January 18, 1871, when William Frederick Louis (William I or Wilhelm I) officially became the first German Emperor. Therefore, from July 1, 1867 to January 18, 1871, makes a total of 42 months: three years and six months.

The prophecy, concerning **"one of his heads"** was **"wounded to death"** (Revelation 13:3) was fulfilled when the "Holy Roman Empire of the German Nation," was dissolved in 1806. This scripture is talking about the "coat of arms" (the "Two Headed Black Eagle"), which represented the "Holy Roman Empire," for many centuries. In 1871, after the "Holy Roman Empire of the German Nation" was resurrected, by William Frederick Louis, this "coat of arms" was officially changed to a black eagle with only one head. The **"deadly wound was healed"** (Revelation 13:3), in 1870, when Pope Pius IX declared that the Catholic Church was the "Roman Republic," which remains on earth, today, through the hands of the Pope and "Holy Roman Catholic Church."

The "Book of Revelation" talks about the **"dragon which gave power unto the beast."**

> **"And he opened his mouth in blasphemy against God, to**

blaspheme his name, and his tabernacle, and them that dwell in heaven. And it was given unto him to make war with the saints, and to overcome them: and power was given him over all kindreds, and tongues, and nations. And all that dwell upon the earth shall worship him, whose names are not written in the book of life of the Lamb slain from the foundation of the world"** (Revelation 13:6-8).

This prophecy: **"And he opened his mouth in blasphemy against God, to blaspheme his name, and his tabernacle, and them that dwell in heaven"** is referring to the official Catholic doctrine, concerning "Papal Infallibility." Pope Pius IX introduced, "Papal Infallibility," during the First Vatican Council (1869-1870). This doctrine is blasphemy, against God, because no person on earth is infallible: *only* God is infallible and *only* God is perfect. This declaration is no different than what the Caesars would often proclaim, when they declared that they were superior to every god, that existed. The prophecy: **"And it was given unto him to make war with the saints, and to overcome them: and power was given him over all kindreds, and tongues, and nations"** is referring to the official Catholic doctrine, which is taught by the Pope, around the world. When this scripture says: **"And it was given unto him to make war with the saints, and to overcome them,"** this is talking about the religious disagreements: the "war of words," and the "war of religious doctrines," which exist in modern times. The fact that so many people believe in the Catholic Church doctrine, makes it rather difficult for the saints to overcome its teachings, and win. The prophecy: **"And all that dwell upon the earth shall worship him, whose names are not written in the book of life of the Lamb slain from the foundation of the world"** is simply a warning to the people who continue to worship the Pope, and the "Holy Roman Catholic Church."

Daniel 7:23, **"Thus he said, The fourth beast shall be the** fourth kingdom upon earth, which shall be diverse from all kingdoms, and shall devour the whole earth, and shall tread it down, and break it in pieces."

Interpretation: this verse is explaining that this fourth kingdom (fourth beast) is the "Holy Roman Empire," which was **"diverse from all kingdoms,"** because it was comprised of many different races, cultures, and languages. The prophecy: **"and shall devour the whole earth, and shall tread it down, and break it in pieces,"** is referring to the "Holy Roman Catholic Church" and the doctrine that it teaches, around the world. Understand; the first "Holy Roman Empire" never conquered the entire world. Therefore, the power of the "Holy Roman Empire" was limited to the territories, which its armies could reach. However, the "Holy Roman Catholic Church" is different, simply because the doctrine that the Catholic Church teaches has no boundaries, which means that their doctrine is taught around the world.

Daniel 7:24, "And the ten horns out of this kingdom are ten kings that shall arise: and another shall rise after them; and he shall be diverse from the first, and he shall subdue three kings."

Interpretation: this prophecy: **"And the ten horns out of this kingdom are ten kings that shall arise"** is referring to the "ten kings," from within the "Confederation of the Rhine," who would eventually join the German Confederation. The prophecy: **"and another shall rise after them; and he shall be diverse from the first, and he shall subdue three kings"** is referring to the second horn (William Frederick Louis), who was quite different from the first horn (Augustus Caesar), because this second horn (William Frederick Louis) was not a Roman citizen: **"and he shall be diverse from the first."** The three kings subdued were: Denmark in 1866; Austria in 1866; and France in 1870-1871. To fully understand these prophecies requires that you also understand that even though the "Holy Roman Empire" was unified, when Charlemagne was crowned in 800 A.D., the official "coat of arms" was still a "Two Headed Black Eagle." The prophecy, concerning **"one of his heads was wounded to death"** was not fulfilled, until after the "Holy Roman Empire of the German Nation" was defeated in battle, in 1805, by Napoleon.

In the next verse, we learn more about the third "horn," who was scheduled to come to power.

> **Daniel 7:25, "And he shall speak great words against the most High, and shall wear out the saints of the most High, and think to change times and laws: and they shall be given into his hand until a time and times and the dividing of time."**

Interpretation: when this prophecy is compared, with the historical record, we learn that this prophecy was fulfilled by Pope Pius IX. It was during the First Vatican Council, in 1869-1870, when he introduced the doctrine of "Papal Infallibility." Even though this doctrine caused some contention, among the Bishops, this doctrine was overwhelmingly passed, and became the official doctrine of the Catholic Church, from that time forward. Therefore, it was the Pope's usurp of power, which fulfilled the prophecy: **"and he shall speak great words against the most High, and shall wear out the saints of the most High, and think to change times and laws."** It was also Pope Pius IX who changed the "ten commandments," when he removed the second commandment (the making of idols) and divided the "tenth commandment" ("not to covet") to create the "ninth" and "tenth" commandments. When you compare the Catholic version of the "Ten Commandments," with the Protestant version, or with the King James Version (Exodus 20:3-17), you can see these differences. The reason why the saints **"shall be given into his hand,"** is because the Catholic doctrine is very difficult to overcome, and not easily defeated. This "war of doctrines" (or "war of words") will continue, until Jesus returns, to begin his millennial rule on earth. The different Popes were predicted, to remain in power, for many centuries: **"until a time and times and the dividing of time."**

> **Daniel 7:26, "But the judgment shall sit, and they shall take away his dominion, to consume and to destroy it unto the end."**

Interpretation: this is when the Catholic Church will also be judged.

> **Daniel 7:27, "And the kingdom and dominion, and the greatness of the kingdom under the whole heaven, shall be given to the people of the saints of the most High, whose kingdom is an everlasting kingdom, and all dominions shall serve and obey him."**

Interpretation: the "Kingdom of God" will officially be given unto **"the people of the saints of the most High."** This is when the saints of the "Most High God," will rule the world with Jesus Christ, and every dominion will serve and obey Jesus Christ, from that time forward.

> **Daniel 7:28, "Hitherto is the end of the matter. As for me Daniel, my cogitations much troubled me, and my countenance changed in me: but I kept the matter in my heart."**

Interpretation: even though these prophecies still bothered Daniel, greatly, he kept it to himself. The statement: **"Hitherto is the end of the matter,"** is referring to the fact that this is the last prophecy, concerning the people on earth.

WHY JESUS WAITED UNTIL HE WAS 30

EARLIER WE DISCUSSED that Jesus was about 30 years old when he was baptized (Luke 3:21-23). To fully understand why Jesus waited, until he was 30, can only be understood after we compare the ministry of "John the Baptist," with the ministry of Jesus. It needs to be understood that the age restrictions, concerning the holy priesthood, played a very important role in both ministries. The fact that we see the father of "John the Baptist," who was Zacharias, burning incense in the temple (Luke 1:5-9), not only proves that Zacharias was a High Priest, but it also proves that he was a direct descendant of Aaron.

In the following scriptures, we learn that Aaron, was commanded to burn the incense in the temple:

> "And Aaron shall burn thereon sweet incense every morning: when he dresseth the lamps, he shall burn incense upon it. And when Aaron lighteth the lamps at even, he shall burn incense upon it, a perpetual incense before the Lord throughout your generations" (Exodus 30:7-8).

The phrase **"throughout your generations,"** simply meant that the

High Priests, beginning with Aaron, would continue to perform this priesthood duty inside the temple. The fact that Zacharias was a High Priest, performing this same duty inside the temple, confirms that he was also **"called after the order of Aaron."**

We learn from Luke (Luke 1:5), that John's mother was one of the "daughters of Aaron," which proves that she was also a direct descendant of Aaron. In other words, "John the Baptist" was a direct descendant of Aaron, through the lineage of both parents. This lineage requirement was very important, during biblical times, because in accordance with the priesthood law, only a direct descendant of Aaron could perform the duties of a high priest: **"And no man taketh this honour unto himself, but he that is called of God, as was Aaron"** (Hebrews 5:4). Therefore, it was also through this priesthood law, which allowed "John the Baptist" to begin his ministry in 27 A.D. The fact that both parents were direct descendants of Aaron, provides proof that "John the Baptist" met the necessary lineage requirements, which allowed him to be **"called after the order of Aaron."**

In comparison, Jesus was born in the "House of Judah" (or Juda), which proves that he was not a direct descendant of Aaron, or from the "House of Levi." This means that Jesus would not be able to meet the necessary lineage requirements, which would allow him to perform the duties of a high priest, within the Aaronic Priesthood (the lesser priesthood). In the "Book of Exodus," chapter 28, we learn that Moses gave the tribe of Levi ("House of Levi") the priesthood authority. In the following scripture, we learn that the "House of Judah" (or Juda) never received any priesthood authority, from the hands of Moses:

> **"For it is evident that our Lord sprang out of Juda; of which tribe Moses spake nothing concerning priesthood"** (Hebrews 7:14).

However, there was still one more way for Jesus to receive the priesthood authority, before he begins his ministry. The fact that the "higher priesthood" did not have any lineage requirements attached, also meant that Jesus would qualify to receive this priesthood authority, as soon as he met the necessary age requirements, as explained in the following scripture:

"From thirty years old and upward even until fifty years old, all that enter into the host, to do the work in the tabernacle of the congregation" (Numbers 4:3).

Because the Melchizedek Priesthood (spelled Melchisedec in N.T.) held the necessary authority, to perform the high priest duties inside the temple, also meant that these age restrictions applied to every priesthood holder, during that time. These age restrictions also meant that "John the Baptist" could not perform any high priest duties, inside the temple, until after he turned 30. However, John was still authorized to preach repentance, and baptize. The fact that Jesus had to wait until he was 30 years old, before he could begin his ministry, with the authority of the higher priesthood: **"being called after the order of Melchisedec"** (Hebrews 5:10), should explain why Jesus decided to wait until he was about 30, before he was baptized (Luke 3:21-23). Therefore, Jesus began his ministry as soon as he was baptized, and after he received the higher priesthood: **"being called after the order of Melchizedek."**

In the following scriptures we learn that Jesus obeyed the ancient priesthood laws, which were in effect, during his time:

"And no man taketh this honour unto himself, but he that is called of God, as was Aaron. So also Christ glorified not himself to be made as high priest; but he that said unto him, Thou are my Son, today have I begotten thee. And he saith also in another place, Thou art a priest forever after the order of Melchisedec," (Hebrews 5:4-6).

Who was Melchizedek?

In the New Testament, we learn that Melchizedek (Melchisedec) was the King of Salem, who blessed Abraham after he returned from the slaughter of the kings (Hebrews 7:1-2). This is also when Abraham paid his tithes (a tenth part of all) to him. From this point, most ministers cannot explain what important role that Melchizedek plays, in modern times, or even explain why the holy priesthood was named after him. As a result, they continue to misinterpret, the following scripture:

> **"Without father, without mother, without descent, having neither beginning of days, nor end of life; but made like unto the Son of God; abideth a priest continually"** (Hebrews 7:3).

It needs to be understood that this verse is not talking about Melchizedek, as a physical human being, but is talking about the holy priesthood that Melchizedek held, which was later named: **"after the order of Melchizedek."**

Therefore, it needs to be understood that when this verse says: **"Without father, without mother, without descent, having neither beginning of days, nor end of life,"** this is explaining that the holy priesthood is eternal, which existed with God before the creation. We learn more about this holy priesthood in the following scriptures:

> "And again, my brethren, I would cite your minds forward to the time when the Lord God gave these commandments unto his children; and I would that ye should remember that the Lord God ordained priests, after his holy order, which was after the order of his Son, to teach these things unto the people. And those priests were ordained after the order of his Son, in a manner that thereby the people might know in what manner to look forward to his Son for redemption. And this is the manner after which they were ordained— being called and prepared from the foundation of the world according to the foreknowledge of God, on account of their exceeding faith and good works; in the first place being left to choose good or evil; therefore they having chosen good, and exercising exceedingly great faith, are called with a holy calling, yea, with that holy calling which was prepared with, and according to, a preparatory redemption for such. And thus they have been called to this holy calling on account of their faith, while others would reject the Spirit of God on account of the hardness of their hearts and blindness of their minds, while, if it had not been for this they might have had as great privilege as their brethren. Or in fine, in the first place they were on the same standing with their brethren; thus this holy calling being prepared from the foundation of the world for such as would not harden their hearts, being in and through the atonement of the Only Begotten Son, who was prepared-- And thus being called by this holy calling, and ordained unto the high priesthood of the holy order of God, to teach his commandments unto the children of men, that they also might enter into his rest. This high priesthood being after the order of his Son, which

order was from the foundation of the world; or in other words, being without beginning of days or end of years, being prepared from eternity to all eternity, according to his foreknowledge of all things. Now they were ordained after this manner being called with a holy calling, and ordained with a holy ordinance, and taking upon them the high priesthood of the holy order, which calling, and ordinance, and high priesthood, is without beginning or end Thus they become high priests forever, AFTER THE ORDER OF THE SON, THE ONLY BEGOTTEN OF THE FATHER, who is without beginning of days or end of years, who is full of grace, equity, and truth. And thus it is. Amen. (Alma 13:1-9)

Notice that this scripture says that the high priests were once called **"after the order of the Son, the Only Begotten of the Father."** The holy priesthood was later named after Melchizedek, because of the great things that Melchizedek accomplished, when he was the King of Salem. We learn more about Melchizedek in the following scriptures:

> "Now this Melchizedek was a king over the land of Salem; and his people had waxed strong in iniquity and abomination; yea, they had gone astray; they were full of all manner of wickedness; But Melchizedek having exercised mighty faith, and received the office of the high priesthood according to the holy order of God, did preach repentance unto his people. And behold, they did repent; and Melchizedek did establish peace in the land in his days; therefore he was called the prince of peace, for he was the king of Salem; and he did reign under his father" (Alma 13:17-18).

In other words, Melchizedek was born a human (just like everyone else), who later received the authority of the "higher priesthood," and became a High Priest, which also explains why Abraham paid his tithes to him.

The Truth about the Rapture

When we compare Mr. Millers theory, with what is presently taught in modern times, most Christians should recognize Mr. Miller's theory, as just another prediction for when the "rapture" would occur. We learn more about the "rapture" from the following scriptures:

> **"For the Lord himself shall descend from heaven with a shout, with the voice of the archangel, and with the trump of God: and the dead in Christ shall rise first: then we which are alive and remain shall be caught up together with them in the clouds, to meet the Lord in the air: and so shall we ever be with the Lord"** (1 Thessalonians 4:16-17).

To make this prophecy easier to understand, we will now separate this prophecy, in the following manner:

1. "For the Lord himself shall descend from heaven with a shout, with the voice of the archangel, and with the trump of God:"
2. "and the dead in Christ shall rise first:"
3. "Then we which are alive and remain shall be caught up together with them in the clouds, to meet the Lord in the air:"

4. "and so shall we ever be with the Lord."

Notice that the "rapture" is not scheduled to occur until after **"the Lord himself shall descend from heaven with a shout."**

The next event is when the first resurrection begins: **"the dead in Christ shall rise first."**

Only after the first resurrection is completed: **"the dead in Christ shall rise first"** is when the next event will be fulfilled: **"Then we which are alive and remain shall be caught up together with them in the clouds, to meet the Lord in the air."** In other words, Jesus will **"descend from heaven with a shout,"** which will then begin the first resurrection, and after this first resurrection is completed, is when the people living on earth, will **"meet the Lord in the air."**

Therefore, the whole concept that some people will suddenly disappear, while others will be left behind, is a total fallacy. I guarantee that everyone will know when Jesus returns because: **"the Lord himself shall descend from heaven with a shout,"** and they will also see: **"the heaven departed as a scroll when it is rolled together."** How would it be possible for people living on earth, during that time, not to see these events? In fact, we are also told that many people will choose to hide in the dens, and in the rocks of the mountains, when Jesus arrives:

> **"And the heaven departed as a scroll when it is rolled together; and every mountain and island were moved out of their places. And the kings of the earth, and the great men, and the rich men, and the chief captains, and the mighty men, and every bondman, and every free man, hid themselves in the dens and in the rocks of the mountains; And said to the mountains and rocks, Fall on us, and hide us from the face of him that sitteth on the throne, and from**

the wrath of the Lamb: For the great day of his wrath is come; and who shall be able to stand"** (Revelation 6:14-17)?

There are so many ministers who teach their congregations that Christians will not have to suffer through the "Great Tribulation," because the "rapture" will occur, before the "Great Tribulation" begins. Once again, this is another false theory, which will cause many Christians not to recognize the signs that the "Great Tribulation" has begun. Because so many Christians have been taught that the "rapture" will occur, before the "Great Tribulation" begins, will also cause many Christians to lose their faith in God, during that time. The Christian ministers, who teach this false theory, have completely ignored the following scriptures:

> "But in those days, after that tribulation, the sun shall be darkened, and the moon shall not give her light, And the stars of heaven shall fall, and the powers that are in heaven shall be shaken. and then shall they see the son of man coming in the clouds with great power and glory. and then shall he send his angels, and shall gather together his elect from the four winds, from the uttermost part of the earth to the uttermost part of heaven" (Mark 13:24-27).

To make this scripture easier to understand, we will now separate this prophecy, in the following manner:

1. "But in those days, after that tribulation, the sun shall be darkened, and the moon shall not give her light,"
2. "And the stars of heaven shall fall, and the powers that are in heaven shall be shaken."
3. "and then shall they see the son of man coming in the clouds with great power and glory."
4. "and then shall he send his angels, and shall gather together

his elect from the four winds, from the uttermost part of the earth to the uttermost part of heaven."

The most important thing to learn from this prophecy, concerns the fact that **"after that tribulation"** is completed, is when **"the sun shall be darkened, and the moon shall not give her light,"** and **"the stars of heaven shall fall, and the powers that are in heaven shall be shaken."** This is when Jesus will return to earth: **"and then shall they see the son of man coming in the clouds with great power and glory."** After Jesus returns is when: **"then shall he send his angels, and shall gather together his elect from the four winds, from the uttermost part of the earth to the uttermost part of heaven."** Notice that none of these events will even begin to happen until after the "Great Tribulation" is **over**. Therefore, it needs to be understood that a lot of events will have to happen, before the prophecy: **"Then we which are alive and remain shall be caught up together with them in the clouds, to meet the Lord in the air,"** will be fulfilled. The fact that none of these things will even begin to happen, until after the "Great Tribulation" is over, proves that Christians will not be able to escape this terrible period, on earth. In fact, we are also told that this "tribulation" will be so terrible, that God will have to intervene to save his elect:

> **"And except those days should be shortened, there should no flesh be saved: BUT FOR THE ELECT'S SAKE THOSE DAYS SHALL BE SHORTENED"** (Matthew 24:22).

> **"And except that the Lord had shortened those days, no flesh should be saved: BUT FOR THE ELECT'S SAKE, WHOM HE HATH CHOSEN, he hath shortened the days"** (Mark 13:20).

Understand; the "elect" is referring to the priesthood holders: **"whom he hath chosen."**

How would it be possible for the "elect" (the elect of God) to be on earth, during the "Great Tribulation," if the "rapture" already occurred? The fact that God will intervene, during the "Great Tribulation," to save his "elect" from complete destruction, proves that the "rapture" did not occur, before the "Great Tribulation" began. This is what makes the false theories and false interpretations, taught in modern times, so dangerous to Christians. The Christians who believe that the rapture will occur, before the "Great Tribulation," will be caught completely by surprise, when they realize that this terrible time is already upon them. This same thing happened in 1844, when many Christians lost their faith in God, because they were convinced that God turned his back on them. They failed to understand that the whole theory, Mr. Miller presented, was based upon some false interpretation of the scriptures. This same thing will happen again, during the "Great Tribulation," because many Christians will be convinced that God turned his back on them, when they needed him the most. They do not realize that many ministers have misinterpreted the scriptures, concerning the rapture, and when the rapture will be fulfilled. As a result, many Christians will not get on their knees to pray, and ask God for help, during the "Great Tribulation." Even though God will intervene, to protect his elect from complete destruction, this does not mean that his "elect" will not have to suffer like everyone else, during this terrible time. If the "elect" of God will have to suffer, then what does this reveal about the other Christians, who are living on earth, during that time? Do you think that these Christians will be able to escape, and will not have to suffer, during the "Great Tribulation?" This explains why Christians need to get prepared, so they will have the necessary faith, to trust their Heavenly Father when things get rough.

Therefore, you now have a choice. You can choose to completely ignore everything that was written in this book. Or, you can choose to change your life, and begin living your life, strictly obeying God's laws and commandments. The path that you need to follow, to begin your amazing spiritual journey, was fully explained in this book. What you decide to do with this information, and what decision you will make in the future, is in your hands. Nevertheless, I pray that God will watch over you, and help you choose the right path.

I say these things in the name of Jesus Christ... Amen.

Notes